THE BIG SHIFT

Oneness unplugs from the earth

Christine Nelson

First published in 2016.

The Big Shift

Oneness unplugs from the earth

ISBN: 978-1-910986-14-1 (e-book)
ISBN: 978-1-910986-16-5 (paperback)

CN Publishing House

Maxet House, Liverpool Road, Luton, Bedfordshire, LU1 1RS

Visit our website at www.cnpublishinghouse.com

CN Publishing House is a division of Christine Nelson Enterprises "for we have heard him say that this Jesus the Nazarene will tear down this place and will ***change the traditions and customs which Moses handed down to us."***

Acts 6:14

Watch *closely*: I am preparing something **new**; **it's happening now,** ***even as I speak,*** and you're about to see it. I am preparing a way through the desert;

Waters will flow where there had been none.

Isaiah 43:19

CONTENTS

ACKNOWLEDGEMENT

I would like to first acknowledge our PAPA God who is AMAZING, My Big Brother Jesus who is my absolute HERO and by Confidant and intimate friend Holy Spirit who is a GENIUS!!! THE GOD HEAD THE THREE IN ONE I GET TO PARTNER WITH YOU THIS IS INCREDIBLE AND HUMBLING AT THE SAME TIME. Thank you for the all the Heavenly messengers that you send me as I need them. You know all our needs and you provide bountifully.

I would like to thank the partners of the CNMINISTRIES for their continuous support. A big shout to all our students at the CNM Apostolic Equipping Institute whose encouragement has been second to none.

Love you all dearly. You have made full time ministry a joy. Thank you.

Big thanks to Gail Ingram for editing making suggestions helping the readers experience to be enjoyable. Love you my friend. You are wonderful.

Thanks to Pamela Jones who painted the picture that depicts hugely the subtitle of being unplugged from the earth and to Karizmatik design for putting the book cover together.

Thanks to Pura Track for finding time to do the formatting of this book. Thank you for your service, your patience and love.

DEDICATION

I would like to dedicate this book to my mother who brought me up. I am sure it was not easy but her lessons of truth and discipline still helps to align me with the will of God today.

My mum's attitude towards hard work and planning still inspires me. She showed me how to have great taste but how to work towards all my goals one step at a time.

Mummy thank you for all your love, kindness you have shown me throughout the years. Always looking out for me always wanting the best for me. Indeed, a child cannot grow too old for a mother. Thank you for being my mother, never giving up always answering the call.

Love you dearly Mummy.

INTRODUCTION

Structurally when a building shifts due to an earthquake or any form of natural disaster, the results are damaging and can be dangerous as foundations are misaligned and cracks appear. When people say shift, it doesn't always appear to be a good thing. However, since 2011, I have noticed a significant shift in perspective, mindsets and as a direct result an upgrade in authority and limitless living. I prophesy to you that when God says shift He is removing wrong foundations. He is exposing lies that are rooted in information where He is not the original source. This shift is fundamental as it moves you to embrace God's original intention for you.

When God's Hand is uprooting and aligning we most time feel displaced, like, all we thought we knew has been taken away causing vulnerability and most times fear. This fear causes us to hold on to the old, the familiar, as the howling winds of transition blow over us like endless waves. Yet, though this transition seems endless the need to get wisdom and understanding is crucial in order to experience this BIG SHIFT and not be left behind. Proverbs 4:5-9 elaborates: -

> ***'Whatever it takes to gain Wisdom, do it. To gain understanding, do it! Never forget this! Never stray from what I am telling you. If you don't forsake Lady Wisdom, she will protect you.***
>
> ***Love her, and she will faithfully take care of you. Gaining sound judgment is key, so first things first: go after Lady Wisdom! Now, whatever else you do, follow through to understanding.***
>
> ***Cherish her, and she will help you rise above the confusion of life your possibilities will***

open up before you—embrace her, and she will raise you to a place of honor in return. She will provide the finishing touch to your character—grace; she will give you an elegant confidence.' (VOICE)

Wisdom is gained when you know what God is doing and you can apply it to your life. Through your application, you gain understanding. Believe it or not Lady Wisdom is a real spiritual being that directs us in wisdom.

This Big Shift exposes the things we have depended on over God Himself leaving us bound to these things, the systems, mindsets of this world. Our believing these lies imprisons us and prevents us from seeing the Hand of God on our lives.

This book is God's appeal to us to unplug from this earthly dimension so as to begin to rule from our rightful place in the heavenly dimension. Being inheritors of the promises of God. God is encouraging us to leave old patterns and embrace the new patterns.

These new patterns force us to let go of all we held dear that has caused us to live an **earth** to **heaven** saga. Which is not only frustrating it has made us irrelevant, ineffective and unbelieving believers. **Our Lord always works from Heaven to Earth.** This is why we are seated in Heavenly places even though we are visible on earth. Ephesians 2:6 says**.**

> ***'He raised us up with Him and seated us in the heavenly realms with our beloved Jesus the Anointed, the Liberating King. (VOICE)***

WOW!! You see belief in Christ Jesus is what gave us this privileged position of being seated with Him in Heavenly places. When we live our lives from this dimension doing as we see the Father do, speaking as the Father speaks, believing what He says, transformation occurs in our life on earth. IT IS TIME TO SHIFT. IT IS TIME TO LOOK TO HEAVENS IDEOLOGIES AND LAY DOWN HUMAN WISDOM, HUMAN REASONING, WHICH HAS CAUSED US TO LIVE A HUMAN LIFESTYLE RATHER THAN EMBRACE THE TRUTH THAT WE ARE WAY BEYOND HUMAN, LIVING FROM HEAVEN.

PRAY: -

Lord untether me, unplug me from this earth. UNPLUG ME FROM THE WORLD's SYSTEM. Break me free from every wrong mindset by revealing them and their source, every unhealed emotion reveal it with their cause and remedy, every kind of fear with its memory which keeps me imprisoned, break me free from time to Your timeless reality, untether me from human wisdom that dictate my sleep and teach me how to rest, break me free from Pharmacia to divine health, teach me how to relinquish the principles that have governed my finances reap and sow, tithing to living solely in Harvest Time by just doing as I see the Father do, break off the need for food by knowing you are my food, my need for oxygen because you are my Ruach, break off the expectation of death to immortality, break me free from receiving information from the outside in rather than from the inside out, break me free from every form of dependency or any other source than YOU O God. As I read this book O Lord, reveal and help me break free embracing THE MINDSET OF CHRIST ONCE AND FOR ALL. So that I can live out your original intention for the Life of Christ in me on earth. AMEN.

CHAPTER 1

A NEW CREATION

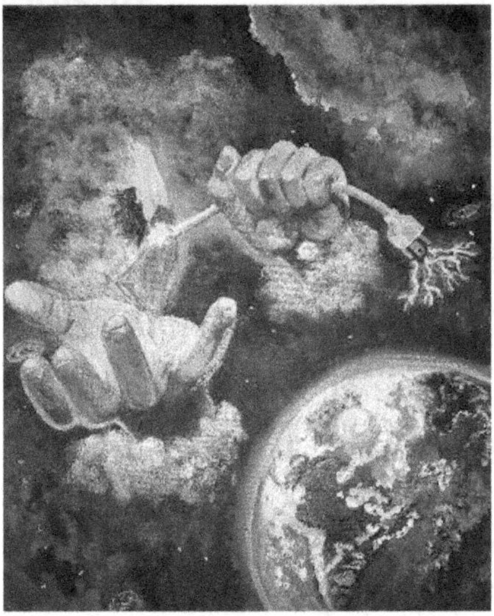

'UNTIL WE REALIZE THAT OUR IDENTITY IS IN CHRIST, THE VEHICLE FOR UNCOMMON FAVOUR, WE WILL CONTINUE TO LOOK TO ALL OTHER AVENUES RATHER THAN THE PATHWAY, THE ULTIMATE DESIGN WE WERE CREATED IN...'

~ CHRISTINE NELSON

2 Corinthians 5:17 says it this way:

> ***Therefore, if anyone is IN CHRIST [that is, grafted in, joined to Him by faith in Him as Savior], he is a new creature [reborn and renewed by the Holy Spirit]; the old things [the previous moral and spiritual condition] have passed away. Behold, new things have come [because spiritual awakening brings a new life. (AMP)***

Being in Christ brings forth a supernatural you a new creature. Causing you and I to manifest all the promises that are associated with being in Christ. The entire Christian walk can only be walked out from the new man as he is awakened.

This new creation is in Christ not in Adam.

- IN HIM we have redemption
- IN HIM we are holy
- IN HIM we are the righteousness of God

- IN HIM we move and have our being
- IN HIM we are more than conquerors
- THROUGH HIM we can do all things
- IN HIM there is no more condemnation
- IN HIM you are no longer a slave but an heir

The phrase NEW CREATION suggests there is an old creation. Being a new creation also implies that this new person you have not yet met because it is the new you. This is not an updated version of you, or a cleaned-up version of you, a new hairstyle of you, or new clothes of you, but a WHOLE NEW CREATION, A NEW YOU.

We are given a new creation because the old man cannot be fixed. It is so whacked, we need to be a NEW CREATION. The fuel that was used to work the old man is fear. The fuel for the new man is love.

The old man is dead! STOP CONSULTING THE OLD MAN - THE OLD MAN IS DEAD! NEW CREATION IS A SUPERNATURAL BIRTH NOT A PHYSICAL BIRTH.

John 1:12-13 says…

> ***But to as many as did receive and welcome Him, He gave the right [the authority, the privilege] to become children of God, that is, to those who believe in (adhere to, trust in, and rely on) His name— who were born, not of blood [natural conception], nor of the will of the flesh [physical impulse], nor of the will of man [that of a natural father], but of God [that is, a divine and supernatural birth—they are born of God—spiritually transformed, renewed, sanctified].***

Created by God, the will of God - not something we inherited, He did not clean us up but created us anew. A brilliant example of this new birth is the supernatural birth of Jesus. In Luke 1:30-38:

> ***Messenger: Mary, don't be afraid. You have found favor with God. Listen, you are going to become pregnant. You will have a son, and you must name Him "Savior," or Jesus. Jesus will become the greatest among men. He will be known as the Son of the Highest God. God will give Him the throne of His ancestor David, and He will reign over the covenant family of Jacob forever.***
>
> ***Mary: But I have never been with a man. How can this be possible?***
>
> ***Messenger: The Holy Spirit will come upon you. The Most High will overshadow you. That's why this holy child will be known, as not just your son, but also as the Son of God. It sounds impossible, but listen—you know your relative Elizabeth has been unable to bear children and is now far too old to be a mother. Yet she has become pregnant, as***

> ***God willed it. Yes, in three months, she will have a son. So the impossible is possible with God.***
>
> ***Mary: (deciding in her heart): Here I am, the Lord's humble servant. As you have said, let it be done to me. VOICE***

This dialogue between the Heavenly Messenger Gabriel and Mary is indelibly what happens when we are born again. The incorruptible seed (eternal seed) of Christ is planted in us concurrently as we decide in our heart to humbly accept the Lordship of Christ over our lives. This incorruptible seed silences all natural DNA from our mother and father. It changes everything as we mature into full grown mature sons of God like Jesus did.

WHO ARE YOU?

- You are not your colour
- You are not your job

- You are not your parents
- You are not your grades
- You are not your weight
- You are not your height
- You are not your behaviour
- You are not the labels you wear or don't wear

Colossians 3:10-11:

> ***...and have put on the new [spiritual] self who is being continually renewed in true knowledge in the image of Him who created the new self— a renewal in which there is no [distinction between] Greek and Jew NATIONALITY, circumcised and uncircumcised (EDUCATION), [nor between nations whether barbarian or Scythian (ETHNICITY), [nor in status whether] slave or free (ECONOMIC STATUS), but Christ is all, and in all [so believers are equal in Christ, without distinction.***

CHRIST IS EVERYTHING!!!

> ***"So from now on we regard no one from a human point of view [according to worldly standards and values]. Though we have known Christ from a human point of view, now we no longer know Him in this way." (2 Corinthians 5:16***

This scripture urges us to NO LONGER PERCEIVE EACH OTHER FROM AN EARTHLY PERSPECTIVE (HUMAN POINT OF VIEW) BE IT BASED ON GENDER, GENETICS, SOCIAL STATUS…or the like. For us to have a new perspective we must embrace the new creation we are.

Colossians 3:4 MSG:

> ***"Your old life is dead. Your new life, which is your real life—even though invisible to spectators—is with Christ in God. He is your***

> ***life. When Christ (your real life, remember) shows up again on this earth, you'll show up, too—the real you, the glorious you. Meanwhile, be content with obscurity, like Christ."***

Colossians 3:4 AMP:

> ***When Christ, who is your life, appears, then you also will appear with Him in glory.***

You are the Holy of Holies (dwelling place of God), Mercy Seat (portable sanctuary of God), Jesus on earth, home of God, Ark of the Covenant, Eden - earth and heaven together... To believe this truth is to SHIFT!! Meditate on this truth until it becomes your reality.

CONTINUING IN HIS WORD

> ***So Jesus was saying to the Jews who had believed Him, "If you abide in My word [continually obeying My teachings and living in accordance with them, then] you are truly My disciples. 32 And you will know the truth [regarding salvation], and the truth will set you free [from the penalty of sin]." (John 8:30-32, AMP)***

Our Lord Jesus makes a distinction here about who is truly a disciple. He outlines that these persons CONTINUE IN HIS WORD OR ABIDE (LIVE OUT) HIS WORD. The mistake we have made is believing that the WORD AND the SCRIPTURES ARE THE SAME - that is far from the truth. The SCRIPTURES, when held in our hands, can be taken from us. However, the word cannot be taken from us because it is God's personal Word to you and I. Though it may be from the scriptures themselves, He has given you a personal revelation of that scripture, and it became the WORD. It is then, written or etched on the tablets of our hearts. His Word becomes a reference point of His love for you and I. A reminder of His protection, His Life in us. The scriptures become the Word when the Word becomes flesh in us.

In John 5:39-40:

> ***You search and keep on searching and examining the Scriptures because you think that in them you have eternal life; and yet it is those [very Scriptures] that testify about Me; and still you are unwilling to come to Me so that you may have life.***

Many like these people Jesus spoke to, knew the scriptures by heart and yet Jesus (THE WORD MADE FLESH) stood before them and they did not recognize Him. Unfortunately, we have made the scriptures a god rather than allow the scriptures themselves to reveal the reality of the WORD that continues to be MADE FLESH.

In John 6:63:

> ***It is the Spirit who gives life; the flesh conveys no benefit [it is of no account]. The words I have spoken to you are spirit and life [providing eternal life]. (Amplified)***

This scripture shows us that His words to us are spirit and life.

Our God is a God of pattern. Throughout scripture the Lord has always spoken from Spirit to spirit to mankind. Speaking DESTINY AND LIFE WHILST TRANSFORMING OUR WRONG MINDSETS, RAVISHING THE HEARTS OF MEN WITH HIS CONSISTENT PURSUSAL OF LOVE, UNTIL MAN

RELINQUISHES HIS FALLEN STATE (ADAMIC STATE) AND EMBRACES THE NEW MAN WITHIN OUR TRUE SELF.

MOSES' perception of himself was that he WAS A STUTTERER: - But then... GOD (THE WORD) showed up and spoke to Moses...

> ***"Who has made man's mouth? Or who makes the mute or the deaf, or the seeing or the blind? Is it not I, the Lord? Now then go, and I, even I, will be with your mouth, and will teach you what you shall say." But he said, "Please my Lord, send the message [of rescue to Israel] by [someone else,] whomever else You will [choose]."***
>
> ***Then the anger of the Lord was kindled and burned against Moses; He said, "Is there not your brother, Aaron the Levite? I know that he speaks fluently. Also, he is coming out to meet you, and when he sees you, he will be overjoyed. You must speak to him and put***

> ***the words in his mouth; I, even I, will be with your mouth and with his mouth, and I will teach you what you are to do. Moreover, he shall speak for you to the people; he will act as a mouthpiece for you, and you will be as God to him [telling him what I say to you]. You shall take in your hand this staff, with which you shall perform the signs [the miracles which prove I sent you]." (Exodus 4 :11-17, AMPLIFIED)***

Listen…as to our God and Father speak faith, confidence, and made provision for Moses in his anxiety and his seem less inadequacies. What is clear by this picture is the ways we see ourselves is a counterfeit version to how our Father sees us. We see ourselves with limitation but our God is speaking profoundly to Moses and to all those he has called to be His mouthpiece. They are: - 1) I am the one who made your mouth knowing full well you would be my mouthpiece. 2) I am not calling you because your perfect eloquent speech, I am calling you because I believe in you. 3)I believe that because you know you are not able to on your own, you will lean into Me to give you every Word because it is not about eloquence but more about being My Representative.

Jacob thought of himself as only a SCHEMER A THIEF AND A LIAR. He had a dream/an encounter, in which he saw a stairway set up on the earth with its top reaching up to heaven. He saw the angels of God going up and coming down on it. The Lord was standing above it, saying,

> ***"I am the Lord, the God of your grandfather Abraham and the God of Isaac. I will give the land on which you are lying to you and your descendants. Your descendants will be like the dust on the earth. You will spread out to the west and to the east, to the north and to the south. Through you and through your***

> ***descendant every family on earth will be blessed. Remember, I am with you and will watch over you wherever you go. I will also bring you back to this land because I will not leave you until I do what I've promised you." Then Jacob woke up from his sleep and exclaimed, "Certainly, the Lord is in this place, and I didn't know it!" Filled with awe, he said, "How awe-inspiring this place is! Certainly, this is the house of God and the gateway to heaven!" (Genesis 28:12-17, EMPHASIS MINE)***

Jacob could only see his wrong behavior. His impure motives that caused him to scheme, manipulate, to lie and concoct plans to ultimately get what he wanted. Jacob was determined to provide for himself and whatever the cost. Even if it meant hurting others. He came to a place where he needed God to change him. He realized, though, he was seemingly wealthy he was empty and he wanted to change from within so his behavior would change. His first encounter with his Creator Face to face he held on to Him for a new and a transformed life. Jacob lived a life of fear which led to shame, guilt and condemnation. Fear told him he had to provide for himself but when the Lord showed up, He showed him the asked him his name and he replied in confession Jacob-Schemer-Liar. But God.... spoke destiny into the old creation Jacob and gave him a new name, new nature, a new character.... You are Israel (Prince of God). In his confession of who he had become by continuously feeding the old man (Adamic nature) he was awakened to a new man the new creation that God desired for him to be, the Prince of God.

The Apostle Paul thought he was a justified MURDERER OF CHRISTIANS

....Now in Damascus there was a disciple named Ananias; and the Lord said to him in a vision, "Ananias." And he answered, "Here I am, Lord." And the Lord said to him, "Get up and go to the street called Straight, and ask at the house of Judas for a man from Tarsus named Saul; for he is praying [there], and in a vision he has seen a man named Ananias come in and place his hands on him, so that he may regain his sight." But Ananias answered, "Lord, I have heard from many people about this man, especially how much suffering and evil he has brought on Your saints (God's people) at Jerusalem; and here [in Damascus] he has authority from the high priests to put in chains all who call on Your name [confessing You as Savior]." But the Lord said to him, "Go, for this man is a [deliberately] chosen instrument of Mine, to bear My name before the Gentiles and kings and the sons of Israel; for I will make clear to him how much he must suffer and endure for My name's sake."

So Ananias left and entered the house, and he laid his hands on Saul and said, "Brother Saul, the Lord Jesus, who appeared to you on the road as you came [to Damascus], has sent me so that you may regain your sight and be filled with the Holy Spirit [in order to proclaim Christ to both Jews and Gentiles]." Immediately something like scales fell from Saul's eyes, and he regained his sight. Then he got up and was baptized; and he took some food and was strengthened.

Saul Begins to Preach Christ

For several days [afterward] Saul remained with the disciples who were at Damascus. And immediately he began proclaiming Jesus in the synagogues, saying, "This Man is the Son of God [the promised Messiah]!" All those who heard him continued to be amazed and said, "Is this not the man who in Jerusalem attacked those who called on this name [of Jesus], and had come here [to Damascus] for the express purpose of bringing them bound [with chains]

> ***before the chief priests?" But Saul increased in strength more and more, and continued to perplex the Jews who lived in Damascus by examining [theological evidence] and proving [with Scripture] that this Jesus is the Christ (the Messiah, the Anointed). Acts 9:11-22***

The Apostle Paul had a remarkable encounter but before Paul could be given new eyes to see himself as the new creation, the prophet Ananias had to change the way he perceived Paul and choose to see Paul through the eyes of Jesus (crucial for any impartation) so as to be a conduit of what the Lord wanted to release in Paul's life. Jesus revealed to Ananias His ultimate purpose and destiny for Paul. Jesus saw all Paul had done and what he was doing and awakened him to God's vision for him as, a new creation.

In Acts 9:4-6:

> ***"Saul, Saul, why are you persecuting and oppressing Me?" And Saul said, "Who are You, Lord?" And He answered, "I am Jesus whom you are persecuting, now get up and go into the city, and you will be told what you must do."***

When Jesus met Paul face to face on the road to Damascus He asked Paul why are you persecuting ME? Jesus saw His people as Himself, no more no less. Jesus revealed to Paul His fierce love for his people that causes Him to relentlessly pursue them. He reveals the oneness He shares with His people that anyone who tries to oppress or persecute His people, is shown in how by Paul's mistreatment of his people he was inevitably doing the same to Him (Jesus). I believe Jesus' love for His people wrecked Paul. He had never known such love and he saw the high regard the people of God were perceived by their Lord and Savior. By this revelation, Paul too desired with a longing the need to be one with Christ too. When Ananias went to meet Paul he spoke as the mouthpiece of God speaking destiny and life, calling forth the gold of the new creation in Paul. He said:

> ***"Brother Saul, the Lord Jesus, who appeared to you on the road as you came [to Damascus], has sent me so that you may regain your sight and be filled with the Holy Spirit [in order to proclaim Christ to both Jews and Gentiles]." Immediately something like scales fell from Saul's eyes, and he regained his sight. Then he got up and was baptized; and he took some food and was strengthened. Saul Begins to Preach Christ. Acts 9:17***

Please note that Ananias did not speak to him like a stranger who was instrumental in killing his brothers but spoke to him as his very own 'brother in Christ.' It speaks volumes of Ananias 'repentance in no longer seeing Paul from an old creation but the new creation that he is. He spoke Paul's destiny as He was instructed and Paul instantly went about doing what God had purposed him to do. His name, nature, character changed as he became Paul (meaning: - small humble) as seen in Acts 13 from Saul (meaning: -asked for prayed for).

THIS BIG SHIFT WE SPEAK OF FROM OLD CREATION TO NEW CREATION OCCURS IN US WHEN THE WORD SPEAKS DESTINY SO PROFOUNDLY INTO OUR LIVES THAT WE CAN NEVER BE THE SAME. Even Jesus needed the Father to speak destiny into Him. We see this on two occasions where the WORD of GOD was released audibly through an open heaven declaring who Jesus is but also alerting to those who stood with Him to HEAR HIM.

> ***"THIS IS MY SON IN WHOM I AM WELL PLEASED" (Matthew 3:17)***

"THIS IS MY SON IN WHOM I AM WELL PLEASED HEAR YE HIM" (Matthew 17: 5)

ARE YOU SEEKING OUT THE WORD OF GOD, THE VOICE OF GOD IN YOUR LIFE? When His Word comes, something must die for the NEW REVEALTORY INSIGHTS to be awakened to the new creation in you.

Confession is needed that is aligned with heaven with every revelation of who you are a change of name occurs.

1. **YOU ARE ONE WITH CHRIST** His number one person. 1 John 4:17b, ***As He is so are you*** (ALL THAT HE IS YOU ARE - TWINS)

2. **YOU ARE HIS PASSION** He isn't interested in being your priority. Psalm 139:17:

'Your thoughts and plans are treasures to me, O God! I cherish each and every one of them! How grand in scope! How many in number!'

3.**YOU ARE HIS EXPRESSION** He isn't trying to control you, but to express you. Jesus said:

> ***"Be of good cheer, I have overcome the world." (John 16:33)***

> ***So we are ambassadors for Christ, as though God were making His appeal through us; we [as Christ's representatives] plead with you on behalf of Christ to be reconciled to God. (2 Corinthians 5:20)***

> "***Beloved, your old, fear-filled self is dead. It has no voice. Your new self in Christ is being raised up so that you can occupy your circumstances completely differently. Listen to who you really are. Let God upgrade your thinking***."

PARADIGM SHIFT ACTIVATION

- OPEN YOUR HEART TO HIM (Be gut honest)
- LET NOTHING PUT YOU OFF, distract you, fix your eyes on Him and Him alone – LOOK TO HIM as your only Source
- BE AT PEACE ABOUT WHO YOU ARE, LET THAT WEARINESS WASH AWAY
- SEE YOURSELF THROUGH HIS EYES
- HE IS FOR YOU, HE IS ON YOUR SIDE, HE loves you so profoundly
- YOU HAVE UNCOMMON FAVOUR WITH YOUR FATHER BECAUSE OF HIS DNA IN YOU
- **'Hear the yes I have said to you because you are the apple of my eye'** says the Lord.

- ALLOW HIM TO ENLIGHTEN YOUR EYES TO BELIEVE WHO YOU ARE IN HIM
- Listen to His Heart as whispers ***"Trust My heart for you - I have set my affections on you. I love who you are - trust in me.***

Embracing the new creation: - move from gifts to love the more excellent way. Testimony of the seven spirits resting on your life fully.

[redacted]

CHAPTER 2

NEW WAY OF THINKING

"THE THOUGHTS YOU DWELL ON IN YOUR HEART CREATE THE PATH YOU WILL WALK ON'

~ CHRISTINE NELSON

Proverbs 23:7

'as a man thinks in his heart so is he'

Thinking in your heart and thinking in your head are two different realms...One realm creates and multiplies while the other creates a hard heart. Moving Godly thoughts from our heads to our hearts by chewing it over by way of meditation is crucial to SHIFTING TO THIS NEW WAY OF THINKING.

I have found that we meditate on many things through singing a song, listening to a conversation, a song, by reading, we naturally meditate as we naturally worry. One could say worry is the negative to meditate. To move from a depraved mind-set requires us to be intentional with what comes out of our mouths whether by singing, talking, listening, reading and so forth. I love the song... "SET A FIRE"

The lyrics are good, along with many other songs, but they don't always reveal the whole truth or reinforce a belief or thought process that the promises of God are in the future not NOW without accepting what is ours TODAY. Please note this is no disrespect to the writers, I am simply highlighting unbelief and how it masquerades itself.

The Lyrics are: - *"set a fire down in my soul that I can't contain that I can't control I want more of you Lord."* It implies a begging and a pleading of a God who is stingy and needs us to whimper before He lifts a hand.

IF WE CHANGE OUR THINKING THAT WE DO NOT HAVE RATHER THAT SPEAK WHAT WE HAVE, The lyrics would be more like this; I HAVE A FIRE DOWN IN MY SOUL THAT I CAN' T CONTAIN THAT I CAN"T CONTROL I HAVE ALL OF YOU, GOD.

Another song, *"I wanna be where you are…"* When Ephesians 2:6 tells us we are ALREADY seated in Heavenly places. So there is no need to beg Him to be where we already are, "I AM WHERE YOU ARE".

"Holy Spirit come" is another song that comes to mind, the Holy Spirit, is always with you, He never leaves you. Begging Him to come is unbelief. *"Thank you, Holy Spirit, that you are always here with me help me to be more aware of your presence*", is probably a better statement.

NOTICE THE CHANGE IN LYRICS SPEAKS TRUTH AND INEVITBALY INCREASE FAITH RATHER THAN THE STANCE OF ASKING FOR WHAT WE ALREADY HAVE. THERE ARE TWO TYPES OF PRAYERS GOD CANNOT ANSWER,

1) THE PRAYERS THAT ARE AGAINST HIS WILL

2) PRAYERS OF UNBELIEF, ASKING FOR WHAT WE ALREADY HAVE.

Hebrews 3 highlights the reality that the biggest problem in the world is not drugs, curse words, churches, religion, lying, stealing, homosexuality, transgender, smoking, etc. THE BIGGEST PROBLEM IS UNBELIEF!

Unbelief is the cause of all those things......The things we do or fail to do is because we have failed to believe, trust, rely on the Lord. Faith, trust, obedience through reliance are the only things that bring us into a place of REST. REST IS THE ONLY POSITION OF POWER, HIS REST IS AN OFFENSIVE WEAPON AGAINST SATAN.

"Take care, brothers and sisters, that there not be in any one of you a wicked, unbelieving heart [which refuses to trust and rely on the Lord, a heart] that turns away from the living God. But continually encourage one another every day, as long as it is called "Today" [and there is an opportunity], so that none of you will be hardened [into settled rebellion] by the deceitfulness of sin [its cleverness, delusive glamour, and sophistication]. For we [believers] have become partakers of Christ [sharing in all that the Messiah has for us], if only we hold firm our newborn confidence [which originally led us to Him] until the end, while it is said, "Today [while there is still opportunity] if you hear His voice, Do not harden your heart, as when they provoked Me [in the rebellion in the desert at Meribah]."

For who were they who heard and yet provoked Him [with rebellious acts]? Was it not all those who came out of Egypt led by Moses? And with whom was He angry for

forty years? Was it not with those who sinned, whose dead bodies were scattered in the desert? And to whom did He swear [an oath] that they would not enter His rest, but to those who disobeyed [those who would not listen to His word]? So we see that they were not able to enter [into His rest—the promised land] because of unbelief and an unwillingness to trust in God. Hebrews 3:12-19

When He speaks faith into us and we resist by settling for unbelief. we are hardening our hearts, as we silence His voice to us. If we cannot believe His Word we cannot be who He says we are. Our thoughts will be depraved. Stinking thinking causes to create negatively, rather than being the co-creators, co-heirs of God that we are.

TEMPORAL MINDSETS

This new way of thinking requires TEMPORAL MINDSETS to be uprooted. Temporal mind-sets keep us insecure, afraid, with an unwillingness to be wholehearted about anything. No one commits wholeheartedly to something that WILL potentially dissipate at some point.

If our thoughts concerning our adoption by God was temporary, we would NOT be able to love the Lord God with all our heart, soul and strength. Nor will be able to seek Him with all our hearts and according to scripture this is the ONLY way to find Him. We would always withhold parts of our hearts. The truth is, temporal mind-sets are so ingrained in us that we naturally find it hard to give of ourselves fully. We cower in fear. Our Father loves us so that He Himself little by little reveals to us our fears which in turn releases us to love more. Temporal mind-sets are at the heart of all insecurities and affects greatly the extent we can love our God, and yet He encourages us to do everything with all our hearts.

We see a brilliant example of settling for the temporary rather than contending for the eternal in story of ESAU AND JACOB. Esau gave up his innate eternal birthright to gratify a temporary hunger because he was thinking of his immediate growling stomach. A temporal mindset causes us to make an eternal decision when we are faced with a temporary situation. This does not make us dangerous to ourselves but to others.

Everything Jesus has done for us has eternal implications. He does this to build our faith in an eternal God who is faithful, trustworthy and is worthy of our trust. An eternal mindset removes the failings of insecurity, doubt, worry, in God who is INCAPABLE of letting us down when our faith is anchored in Him alone.

> ***For the death that He died, He died to sin [ending its power and paying the sinner's debt] ONCE AND FOR ALL; and the life that He lives, He lives to [glorify] God [IN UNBROKEN FELLOWSHIP WITH HIM]. (Romans 6:10)***

> ***AND TO JESUS, THE MEDIATOR OF A NEW COVENANT [UNITING GOD AND MAN], and to the sprinkled blood, which speaks [of mercy], a better and nobler and more gracious message than the blood of Abel [which cried out for vengeance]. (Hebrews 12:24)***

> ***how much more will the blood of Christ, who through the eternal [Holy] Spirit willingly offered Himself unblemished [that is, without moral or spiritual imperfection as a sacrifice] to God, CLEANSE YOUR CONSCIENCE FROM DEAD WORKS AND LIFELESS***

OBSERVANCES TO SERVE THE EVER LIVING GOD? (Hebrews 9:14)

We can say that Jesus came to eradicate that which was temporary and to establish a better and a more excellent way, an eternal way through His blood no longer the blood of animals, from His priesthood the order of Melchizedek not the Aaronic priesthood. His blood speaks of our eternal righteousness. Therefore, the temporal mindsets we have upheld are in opposition to the nature of God and opposes the eternal sacrifice that was made on the cross and consequentially our inheritance that was given to us.

To embrace an eternal mindset will also crucify a death driven mentality.

"For God so [greatly] loved and dearly prized the world, that He [even] gave His [One and]

> ***only begotten Son, so that whoever believes and trusts in Him [as Savior] shall not perish, but have eternal life. (John 3:16)***

> ***"I assure you and most solemnly say to you, the person who hears My word [the one who heeds My message], and believes and trusts in Him who sent Me, has (possesses now) eternal life [that is, eternal life actually begins—the believer is transformed], and does not come into judgment and condemnation, but has passed [over] from death into life." (John 5:24)***

> ***The world is passing away, and with it its lusts [the shameful pursuits and ungodly longings]; but the one who does the will of God and carries out HIS PURPOSES LIVES FOREVER. (1 John 2:17)***

To take on an eternal mindset is to also not allow conclusions to prevent us from gaining access to further revelation. An eternal mindset tells us there is always more. Refusing to put a full stop where our eternal God has put a comma, a semi colon, or an ellipsis.

> ***To those who by persistence in doing good seek [unseen but certain heavenly] glory, honor, and IMMORTALITY, [HE WILL GIVE THE GIFT OF ETERNAL LIFE. (Romans 2:7)***

DUAL MINDSETS

Dual mindsets keep you double-minded, indecisive, going around in circles but going nowhere.

> ***But he must ask [for wisdom] in faith, without doubting [God's willingness to help], for the one who doubts is like a billowing surge of the sea that is blown about and tossed by the wind. For such a person ought not to think or expect that he will receive anything [at all] from the Lord, 8 being a double-minded man, unstable and restless in all his ways [in***

> ***everything he thinks, feels, or decides]. (James 1:6-7)***

This kind of mindset is directly connected to eating from the tree of good and evil. Today we are faced with the same choices as Adam and Eve, will we choose the Tree of life which is Jesus Himself bringing abundant life or the tree of knowledge good and evil that brought about double mindedness along with the continuous oppression and killing of the spirit man. Any thought, word or deed that causes your spirit man to die, is as a result of partaking from the fruit of the tree of good and evil.

This dual mindset gives birth to a RELIGIOUS MINDSET –

- speaking to our children anyway but you speak respectfully to your Pastor
- Judging others because they sin differently

- Living a double lifestyle

RELIGIOUS MINDSETS GIVE BIRTH TO A SLAVERY MENTALITY: - that tells us, we are not good enough only PASTORS CAN, BISHOPS CAN, ONLY PROPHETS CAN, ONLY DO IF YOU ARE TOLD and also you have to be chastised or WHIPPED BEFORE THEY LEARN THEIR LESSON.

This same dual mindset, that leads to a religious spirit leads to a PERFORMANCE MINDSET. Performance mindset is not motivated by love but by selfish ambition that impurely motivates causing wrong intentions. It tells you, you have to do something before God will bless you or lift a hand to help you. IT thrives so much on works that insecurity is developed. It dictates to us, to settle for SHOWING OFF A SKILL, RATHER THAN EMPOWERING OTHERS TO DO WHAT YOU

DO. IS IT ONLY FOR YOU? Performance mindset will take a large vision and cause you to be nearsighted seeing only me, myself and I.

SHIFT TO THE MIND OF CHRIST!!

> ***For who has known the mind and purposes of the Lord, so as to instruct Him? But we have the mind of Christ to be guided by His thoughts and purposes. (1 Corinthians 2:16)***

The Apostle Paul writes to the Philippian church imploring them to BE LIKE CHRIST AS THEY PUT ON THE MIND OF CHRIST.

> ***Therefore, if there is any encouragement in Christ, if there is any consolation of love, if there is any fellowship of the Spirit, if any affection and compassion, make my joy complete by being of the same mind, maintaining the same love, united in spirit, intent on one purpose. Do nothing from***

selfishness or empty conceit, but with humility of mind regard one another as more important than yourselves; do not merely look out for your own personal interests, but also for the interests of others. Have this attitude in yourselves which was also in Christ Jesus, who, although He existed in the form of God, did not regard equality with God a thing to be grasped, but emptied Himself, taking the form of a bond-servant, and being made in the likeness of men. Being found in appearance as a man, He humbled Himself by becoming obedient to the point of death, even death on a cross. For this reason also, God highly exalted Him, and bestowed on Him the name which is above every name, so that at the name of Jesus every knee will bow, of those who are in heaven and on earth and under the earth, and that every tongue will confess that Jesus Christ is Lord, to the glory of God the Father. (Philippians 2:1-11)

MIND OF CHRIST IS ONE WITH THE WILL OF GOD

When you read the passage above it highlights to us the heart of Christ, as His mindset is revealed. This is what I perceive as I see the mind of Christ becomes one with the will of God. "I go to do your will, Father." Indeed, Jesus determined ahead of time, "I am laying down my will in order to do yours, Father. I subjugate my will so that I may embrace yours. Everything I say and do has to come from you. I'm laying down everything to be totally dependent upon you." The Father's agreement with the Son was to reveal his will to Him. God said to Him, in essence, "My will won't ever be hidden from you. You will always know what I am doing. You will have my mind."

When we do not have His mind in us we fall prey to the natural behaviors of this world, rather than aligning with His will.

- Those who tackle their insecurities with humour.
- Those who wrap themselves in positivity and pretend they have no insecurities.
- Those who verbally (and constantly) doubt themselves and put themselves down.
- Those who make up all sorts of fabulous stories and tales about themselves that aren't true.
- Is consciously aware of the invisible God and does all in honor of Him - the mind of Christ does not do because everyone else is watching or not watching

MIND OF CHRIST LACKS NOTHING

It does not focus on what it does not have. Hence complaining and murmuring is out of the question.

Do everything without murmuring or questioning [the providence of God], 15 so that you may prove yourselves to be blameless and guileless, innocent and uncontaminated, children of God without blemish in the midst of a [morally] crooked and [spiritually] perverted generation, among whom you are seen as bright lights [beacons shining out clearly] in the world [of darkness], 16 holding out and offering to everyone the word of life, so that in the day of Christ I will have reason to rejoice greatly because I did not run [my race] in vain nor labor without result. 17 But even if I am being poured out as a [d]drink offering on the sacrifice and service of your faith [for preaching the message of salvation], still I rejoice and share my joy with you all. 18 You too, rejoice in the same way and share your joy with me. (Philippians 2:14-18)

ALIGN WITH THE MIND OF CHRIST

- The mind of Christ does not reason, is not operating from earthly logic.
- The mind of Christ walks blind and deaf so it can hear and see.
- The mind of Christ does not have to know all the details, one instruction from the Father is enough.
- The mind of Christ renews vision, restores faith, realigns us with the pathways of God, reinstates faith that is fully persuaded.
- Let His mind be in you.

PARADIGM SHIFT ACTIVATION

BELIEVE: STOP BEING AN UNBELIEVER IF JESUS DID IT, SAID IT, BELIEVE IT. (HE IS THE SOURCE OF ALL TRUTH).

REST: THIS REST ACTIVELY SEEKING OUT HIS HEART, WILL, MIND AND EMOTIONS.

MANIFEST: YOU WILL DO GREATER THINGS THAN JESUS DID (John 14:12).

CHAPTER 3

NEW AUTHORITY

"HIS AUTHORITY LOOKS GOOD ON YOU WHEN YOU ARE CONSCIOUSLY AWARE OF WHO YOU CARRY"

~ CHRISTINE NELSON

The word "**authority**" is translated from the Greek word ***exousia.*** It is denoting ability or strength that one is endued or given. We see that this word is used somewhat interchangeably in the New Testament meaning power or authority depending on its context.

There is a profound distinction between the words power and authority. ***Power is the ability or force to accomplish something while authority is the right to carry it out*** according to dictionary definition. Sometime ago I asked the Lord what the differences are between the two words and I instantly had a picture of someone driving a car in the night and out of nowhere steps a police officer attired in his uniform with his hand out authoritatively stopping the vehicle. I instantly sensed the Lord saying to me that authority is worn. I began to ask myself if I would stop in the middle of the night if a police man who had on plain clothes stopped me, without any visible signs of his authority....

'**POWER ON THE OTHER HAND, IS FROM WITHIN**,' the Lord explained to me. I asked for an example and I was reminded of the power of the Holy Spirit that dwells within us but also His authority that clothes us.

Saints, our authority is under attack if we allow the things of this world to govern our lives. When we are under the authority of the Lord we are empowered to be anchored in HIS authority. When we are striving to be all that the world deems are stepping stones towards a position of authority we succumb to self-promotion, self-glorification, selfish ambition, self-will and the like. WHEN WE ARE CLOTHED IN HIS AUTHORITY THERE IS A SUPERNATURAL REST THAT PROPELS US TO GO FARTHER,

DEEPER; BUT, FALSE AUTHORITY, STRIVING IS ESSENTIAL.

God's authority on you commands atmospheres to change, vibrations to align with the will of God, motions the heart of God in you to manifest, it generates the healing power of God to heal by His presence resting on you, it causes spiritual senses to be one with Heavens agenda on the earth. It commands the attention of man to an ETERNAL GOD. It convicts, and changes the hearts of those who encounters this authority, it demands reverence and awe of an OMNIPOTENT God as the spirit of the fear of the Lord rests upon you. HIS AUTHORITY looks good on you.

SOME EXAMPLES OF THE EXOUSIA

But I will point out to you whom you should fear: fear the One who, after He has killed, has authority and power to hurl [you] into hell; yes, I say to you, [stand in great awe of God and] fear Him! (Luke 12:5)

When we handle and rightly divide the word of God and are consciously aware of the Spirit of the fear of the Lord we will have the reverence and awe of God to make good choices which empowers us to walk in authority. We strip ourselves of the authority entrusted to us when we begin to add or take away causing us to drift off course and all in fellowship with them are in danger. Whose authority will they act under?

So now through the church the multifaceted wisdom of God [in all its countless aspects] might now be made known [revealing the mystery] to the [angelic] rulers and

> ***authorities in the heavenly places. (Ephesians 3:10)***

According to this example of exousia, we the church the people of God are built with multifaceted wisdom of God and this is revealed as we recognize the heavenly help that has been given to us to rule.

Jesus made it clear throughout the gospels that the word of God is the Source of Authority. He did this by the very Words He uttered before every healing, deliverance or raising the dead. He proved over and over again that HIS WORD in OUR MOUTH, CARRIES HIS AUTHORITY. For us to walk in this authority we too must take on the attitude of that Jesus demonstrated to us.

In John 14:10-14 He said:

"The words I say to you I do not say on My own initiative or authority, but the Father, abiding continually in Me, does His works [His attesting miracles and acts of power]. Believe Me that I am in the Father and the Father is in Me; otherwise believe [Me] because of the [very] works themselves [which you have witnessed]. I assure you and most solemnly say to you, anyone who believes in Me [as Savior] will also do the things that I do; and he will do even greater things than these [in extent and outreach], because I am going to the Father. And I will do whatever you ask in My name as My representative, this I will do, so that the Father may be glorified and celebrated in the Son. If you ask Me anything in My name [as My representative], I will do it.

Jesus explains that He Himself does nothing on His own initiative but as He sees the Father do. He then reassures us that our faith in Him will empower us to do even greater works. WOW! It sounds simple enough. Yet, Nicodemus felt the way many of us do even now. Nicodemus wanted to know how Jesus was doing what He was doing then... If we do not know how He was doing the miracles He did how will we do greater works than He?

In John 3:1-21:

> ***Now there was a man of the Pharisees, named Nicodemus, a ruler of the Jews; this man came to Jesus by night and said to Him, "Rabbi, we know that You have come from God as a teacher; for no one can do these signs that You do unless God is with him." Jesus answered and said to him, "Truly, truly, I say to you, unless one is born again he cannot see the kingdom of God."***
>
> ***Nicodemus *said to Him, "How can a man be born when he is old? He cannot enter a second time into his mother's womb and be born, can he?" Jesus answered, "Truly, truly,***

I say to you, unless one is born of water and the Spirit he cannot enter into the kingdom of God. That which is born of the flesh is flesh, and that which is born of the Spirit is spirit. Do not be amazed that I said to you, 'You must be born again.' The wind blows where it wishes and you hear the sound of it, but do not know where it comes from and where it is going; so is everyone who is born of the Spirit."

Nicodemus said to Him, "How can these things be?" Jesus answered and said to him, "Are you the teacher of Israel and do not understand these things? Truly, truly, I say to you, we speak of what we know and testify of what we have seen, and you do not accept our testimony. If I told you earthly things and you do not believe, how will you believe if I tell you heavenly things? No one has ascended into heaven, but He who descended from heaven: the Son of Man. As Moses lifted up the serpent in the wilderness, even so must the Son of Man be lifted up; so

that whoever believes will in Him have eternal life.

"For God so loved the world, that He gave His only begotten Son, that whoever believes in Him shall not perish, but have eternal life. For God did not send the Son into the world to judge the world, but that the world might be saved through Him. He who believes in Him is not judged; he who does not believe has been judged already, because he has not believed in the name of the only begotten Son of God. This is the judgment, that the Light has come into the world, and men loved the darkness rather than the Light, for their deeds were evil. For everyone who does evil hates the Light, and does not come to the Light for fear that his deeds will be exposed. But he who practices the truth comes to the Light, so that his deeds may be manifested as having been wrought in God."

When I read this passage three things are highlighted to me. How did Jesus do what He did and is still doing?

I CREATE BY USING LIKE FOR LIKE

Jesus points out that He only deals with like for like. Spirit to Spirit. Apple tree bears apples, dog gives birth to baby dogs or puppies, fig tree bear figs. I am sure you are getting my point. In John 3:3 it reads:

> ***"Rabbi (Teacher), we know [without any doubt] that You have come from God as a teacher; for no one can do these signs [these wonders, these attesting miracles] that You do unless God is with him." Jesus answered him, "I assure you and most solemnly say to you, unless a person is born again [reborn from above—spiritually transformed, renewed, sanctified], he cannot [ever] see and experience the kingdom of God."***

Nicodemus confirms that Jesus is first of all able to do what He does because He is from God. God gives birth to gods. Yes you are god because you are His offspring. Acts 17:29:

> ***Forasmuch then as we are the offspring of God, we ought not to think that the Godhead is like unto gold, or silver, or stone, graven by art and man's device.***

He also reiterates that God is with Jesus. Jesus then adds that when someone is born from above, spiritually transformed, renewed, sanctified HE CAN SEE and EXPERIENCE the KINGDOM OF GOD. This BORN FROM ABOVE IS KEY and must be first be established before we can hope to do what Jesus has been doing. Are you seeing and experiencing the Kingdom of God? Are you born again?

Bottom line Spirit gives birth to spirit because of that truth God who is Spirit is able to communicate to your spirit man and show you what is going on in heaven so you can manifest it on the earth. SPIRIT GIVES BIRTH TO SPIRIT.

I DO NOT ACCEPT SECOND HAND INFORMATION

> ***Nicodemus said to Him, "How can these things be possible?" Jesus replied, "You are the [great and well-known] teacher of Israel, and yet you do not know nor understand these things [from Scripture]? I assure you and most solemnly say to you, WE SPEAK ONLY OF WHAT WE [ABSOLUTELY] KNOW AND TESTIFY ABOUT WHAT WE HAVE [ACTUALLY] SEEN [AS EYEWITNESSES]; AND [STILL] YOU [REJECT OUR EVIDENCE AND] DO NOT ACCEPT OUR TESTIMONY (John 3:9-11)***

Jesus pointed out another key point that is crucial to our belief structures. He said He does not accept second hand information. In other words, the source of all His beliefs is directly from the SOURCE God the Father. He points out that He would have to be a FIRST-HAND WITNESS TO SPEAK OF IT. In other words, He does not permit himself to listen to hearsay. He would not repeat anything He heard but He had no personal revelation of it Himself. He explains to Nicodemus that because of this HE LIVES ONLY BY THE TRUTH (REVELATION FROM THE FATHER) He clearly carries this tremendous authority to do what only what His Father in Heaven says and does.

In the Hebrew language, the word for truth is EMET, when the letter Aleph (the letter which symbolizes the invisible God) is taken from the word EMET that word truth becomes dead. When we partake of death it is soul destroying.

It oppresses, imprisons and wounds our emotions and tells us lies about ourselves and causes us to be motivated by shame, guilt and condemnation. While truth sets us free to be motivated by His everlasting, unconditional, incomparable LOVE. It empowers us walk in HIS AUTHORITY for ETERNITY, It equips us to be HIS GREATER WORKS. The key is to discern when you are about to partake of death and to know when it is truth- SOURCED FROM GOD HIMSELF.

Recently while coming back from doing a conference in Germany the Lord began to elaborate on this some more. He pointed out to me that from the beginning this has been a snare. He showed me that when Eve listened and obeyed the serpent she came into agreement with second hand information which led to her spiritual death as well as Adams. Second hand information, is always sourced in an alternate source it is twisted. When Adam spoke to Eve about the trees, Adam spoke to her as God had said to him making that first-hand information. However, their lack of obedience caused to the truth of God's word cost them dearly. Today we are faced with this temptation on a daily basis. Partnering with Truth builds our Spirit man while we dispel lies. In reality, in this shift building our belief system marinated in Truth is key to our spiritual development.

I DO NOT NEGATIVELY JUDGE

Jesus reveals His mandate to us, and since as Jesus is so are we, I reckon we should listen up…It reads:

> ***FOR GOD DID NOT SEND THE SON INTO THE WORLD TO JUDGE AND CONDEMN THE WORLD [THAT IS, TO INITIATE THE FINAL JUDGMENT OF THE WORLD], BUT THAT THE***

WORLD MIGHT BE SAVED THROUGH HIM. WHOEVER BELIEVES AND HAS DECIDED TO TRUST IN HIM [AS PERSONAL SAVIOR AND LORD] IS NOT JUDGED [FOR THIS ONE, THERE IS NO JUDGMENT, NO REJECTION, NO CONDEMNATION]; but the one who does not believe [and has decided to reject Him as personal Savior and Lord] is judged already [that one has been convicted and sentenced], because he has not believed and trusted in the name of the [One and] only begotten Son of God [the One who is truly unique, the only One of His kind, the One who alone can save him]. This is the judgment [that is, the cause for indictment, the test by which people are judged, the basis for the sentence]: the Light has come into the world, and people loved the darkness rather than the Light, for their deeds were evil. For every wrongdoer hates the Light, and does not come to the Light [but shrinks from it] for fear that his [sinful, worthless] activities will be exposed and condemned. But whoever practices truth [and does what is right—morally, ethically,

> ***spiritually] comes to the Light, so that his works may be plainly shown to be what they are—accomplished in God [divinely prompted, done with God's help, in dependence on Him]." (John 3:17-21)***

So, it is fair to say that our mandate is: "*For God sent me His offspring into the world not to judge and condemn the world but that the world might be saved through Christ in me.*"

That tells me then for this to be a reality we cannot negatively judge. Our Father said something one day to me as I was meditating on the wrong someone had done to me and getting increasingly angry. He said, I cannot judge and love. I can only influence those I love. I was convicted then and repented and have continuously endeavoured to live a life of repentance in this area because negative judgement prevents us from being a people of influence hence being able to move in the authority of God. Negative judgment prevents us from believing the best and causes to make assumptions that will prevent us from extending love to another person. Negative judgement fuels offense, resentment, bitterness, and soon hatred. It creates all forms of negative emotions that are soul destroying stripping us of our God given authority to raise the dead, to deliver and to bring healing.

Recently, I had an experience I never want to forget. A friend of a friend at the time had gone into labour at home as she felt led to do so by the Lord. When it was related to me, I was instantly filled with fear. Not long after she haemorrhaged and went into a coma. When I heard the news of the haemorrhaging was saddened but angry! I was so angry I could not pray. I was angry that the baby was born but without a mother to care for her. I was feeling anguish for her husband who I could only imagine the emotional turmoil of regret he too must have felt. I was upset. The day before God's intervention we went before Him as a class, I was teaching. My heart was veiled. I knew I would not be able to pray if I did not repent of my judgement. Suffice to say, I repented of my judgement and so did her friend. In an instant as I repented, I found myself in her brain. I believed and so I declared that the enemy would not be able to stop her brain from functioning as it should. As a class we began to call her forth and declared her brain would work 100% I began to hear the Lord say that 11:11 the next day was that date. So we began to declare that on the 11:11 she would wake up. The next day they did a scan and the doctors announced that she had 100% brain functioning. Her kidney that had failed was now working. We glorified God for this miracle but I was sobered by the impact negative judgements can have on our hearts and how it could cause death because we cannot influence those we have failed to love. The minute I repented I was able to be moved by the love of God for her to heal and to restore enabling me to see what He sees and to follow His instruction. I knew that this woman's heart was right before God whether she heard God or not was not an issue because her motive was purely to obey God in my heart, I knew that God would restore. Glory be to God! The lesson we learnt is to stay clear from negative judgements but also the power of repentance which enables us to honour the person by thinking the best.

PARADIGM SHIFT ACTIVATION

Ask the Holy Spirit to highlight ways in which you have partaking of the first of these three situations listed rather than the more godly situation.

- How have I partaken of LIKE FOR UNLIKE Spirit to flesh hoping to get Spirit results instead of LIKE FOR LIKE?
- What are the areas that you have partaken of second-hand Information rather than FIRST HAND INFORMATION?
- Begin to identify negatively judgements and turn them to POSITIVE JUDGEMENTS.

And repent by doing a divine exchange asking the Holy Ghost for sensitivity to recognize when you have fallen prey to these soul-destroying hook ups.

[redacted]

CHAPTER 4

NEW WORLD

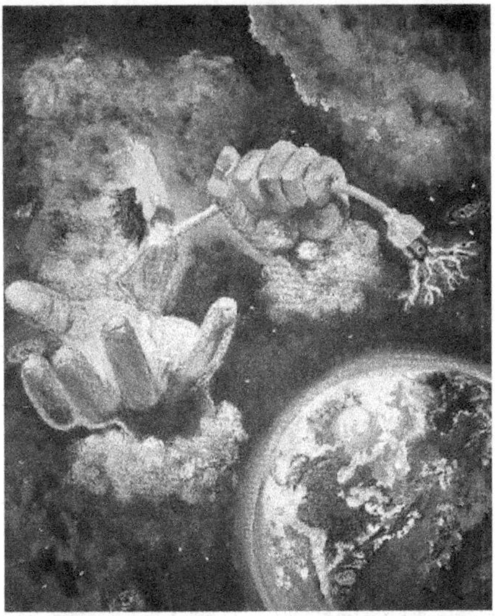

"ONLY HE THAT CAN SEE THE INVISIBLE CAN DO THE IMPOSSIBLE."

~ ANONYMOUS

This Big Shift is so profound that as we begin to embrace our new creation, very quickly we begin to become aware that this world we live in, is an illusion, only a pattern of the real world, new world, the invisible world; THE KINGDOM OF HEAVEN. Jesus spoke more about the Kingdom more than any topic. One could say Jesus came to reveal the Father to us and to establish us as kingdom people.

HE TOLD US WHERE HIS KINGDOM IS..

> ***Jesus said, "My kingdom is not of this world. If it were, my servants would fight to prevent my arrest by the Jews. But now my kingdom is from another place. (John 18:36)***

HE TOLD US HOW TO FIND HIS KINGDOM.

> ***Once, having been asked by the Pharisees when the kingdom of God would come, Jesus replied, "The kingdom of God does not come***

with your careful observation, nor will people say, 'Here it is,' or 'There it is,' because the kingdom of God is within you." (Luke 17:20-21)

JESUS TELLS US THE ATTITUDE OF A CHILD IS KEY TO ENTER HIS KINGDOM.

Little children were brought to Jesus for him to place his hands on them and pray for them. But the disciples rebuked those who brought them. Jesus said, "Let the little children come to me, and do not hinder them, for the kingdom of heaven belongs to such as these." (Matthew 19:13-14)

HE TELLS US WHAT IT WILL TAKE TO SEE THE KINGDOM.

In reply Jesus declared, "I tell you the truth, no one can see the kingdom of God unless he is born again." "How can a man be born when he is old?" Nicodemus asked. "Surely he

> ***cannot enter a second time into his mother's womb to be born!" Jesus answered, "I tell you the truth, no one can enter the kingdom of God unless he is born of water and the Spirit. Flesh gives birth to flesh, but the Spirit gives birth to spirit. You should not be surprised at my saying, 'You must be born again.' (John 3:3-7)***

HE TELLS US WHAT IT WILL TAKE TO ENTER THE KINGDOM

> ***"For I say to you that unless your righteousness (uprightness, moral essence) is more than that of the scribes and Pharisees, you will never enter the kingdom of heaven." Matthew 5:20***

Unfortunately, we have read these scriptures over and over without really having a revelation of them. I believe it is because we have been blinded or deceived by the enemy to believe, that the world we live in is the real world instead of the invisible world, the world within. 2 Corinthians 4:4 says:

> ***among them the god of this world [Satan] has blinded the minds of the unbelieving to prevent them from seeing the illuminating light of the gospel of the glory of Christ, who is the image of God*.**

What is clear about this scripture is that satan lures us through our eyes. Like the religious leaders of Jesus' day, they too did not understand what Jesus meant because the spirit of **religious pride,** that there is nothing they do not know about God because after all they are the religious leaders, spirit of fear of the unknown tells beware of anyone who teaches something different than what you think you know, because you do not want to be deceived. Fear and Pride are huge components.

The Apostle Paul tells us in Ephesians 1:3,

> ***Blessed and worthy of praise be the God and Father of our Lord Jesus Christ, who has blessed us with every spiritual blessing in the heavenly realms in Christ.***

Again, revealing to us that all we need to live this life, all the spiritual blessings are in the HEAVENLY REALMS IN CHRIST.

Unfortunately, to read the scriptures without the Spirit we are not able to see clearly. We perceive with human wisdom rather than heavenly wisdom. True sight is needed for us to embrace the reality of this new world. Jesus tells us these are given to us when we are born again. Born again is a supernatural birth that is of water and Spirit. This is not a physical sight but eyes of the Spirit. True sight is as a result of true knowledge of the Word and sensitivity to the Spirit. The combining force opens our Spiritual eyes through silence or rest. “Be still and know that I am God” Psalm 46:10 says. There is revelation in stillness. There is intimate knowing of God that is revealed in silence.

What kind of a world does God want us to partake of then?

- INVISIBLE
- ETERNAL
- IMMORTAL

Everything we have in the natural we have in the Spirit. Scripture teaches us what is in the spirit is invisible, eternal and is immortal. If we have spiritual eyes then certainly we have spiritual hearing, smell, taste and feelings too. This new world can only be experienced through these five supernatural senses. Jesus said in John 10:27-28:

> ***The sheep that are My own hear My voice and listen to Me; I know them, and they follow Me. And I give them eternal life, and they will never, ever [by any means] perish; and no one will ever snatch them out of My hand.***

This is confirmation of our spiritual ears, which belongs to every sheep or born again believer. Our sense of smell is our ability to discern what is of the soul (mind, will and emotions) or of our Spirit man. Hebrews 4:12 reiterates this:

> ***For the word of God is living and active and full of power [making it operative, energizing, and effective]. It is sharper than any two-edged sword, PENETRATING AS FAR AS THE DIVISION OF THE SOUL AND SPIRIT [THE COMPLETENESS OF A PERSON], AND OF BOTH JOINTS AND MARROW [THE DEEPEST PARTS OF OUR NATURE], EXPOSING AND JUDGING THE VERY THOUGHTS AND INTENTIONS OF THE HEART.***

You see it is the word of God in us, that gives us that discernment of the motives of our hearts, it helps us to judge our thoughts, it reveals the deep things that have become part of us the iniquity of our forefathers that is the joints and marrow.

Our sense of taste manifest as we meditate on what we are partaking of. We not only partake of physical food, but music, information through television, books, someone speaking and so forth. When we partake of anything that is of God we will be able to taste and see that the Lord is good. If it is not God, we will know.

Our feelings comprise of all types of emotion, some negative, some positive. God speak to us through our emotions when we are aware of the oneness we share with Him. We are able to detect the emotions of God Himself and others. You are able to feel the emotions of others even as they physically pass by. Colossians 3: 2-4:

> ***Set your mind and keep focused habitually on the things above [the heavenly things], not on things that are on the earth [which have only temporal value]. FOR YOU DIED [TO THIS WORLD], AND YOUR [NEW, REAL] LIFE IS HIDDEN WITH CHRIST IN GOD. WHEN CHRIST, WHO IS OUR LIFE, APPEARS, THEN YOU ALSO WILL APPEAR WITH HIM IN GLORY.***

Our God is Spirit and He speaks Spirit to spirit. Hence the need for our spiritual senses to be developed. These spiritual senses are accessible as we seek the Lord with all our heart. In this oneness of intimacy, we have access to all that He is, our full inheritance. Unfortunately, if we treat this world we live in as the real world we will continue to choose after the flesh and be EARTHBOUND when we are in fact seated in heavenly places. The truth is we are the ones that decide if we stay earthbound by partaking of the tree of good and evil or the tree of life.

The truth is we partake of sin or we walk in holiness every time this way:

- human senses/spiritual senses
- lust/desire
- action
- incurring consequences.

These four steps open a door based on the path chosen. Unfortunately, the more we make the wrong choices we oppress our spiritual senses and we continue to live a life of deception and illusion. Our choices create for us more of the damnation of this world or opens the door to the NEW WORLD, the Kingdom of Heaven the reality of where we are. We are seated in heavenly places as said in Ephesians 2:6.

Throughout scripture, we see many who naturally lived in dual realms, the Heavenly realm and the Earthly realm. The bible says Enoch walked with God and he was no more. Enoch lived in dual realms and one day He stayed in Heaven and He was no more on the earth.

> ***Jesus answered them by saying, "I assure you and most solemnly say to you, the Son can do nothing of Himself [of His own accord], unless it is something He sees the Father doing; for whatever things the Father does, the Son [in His turn] also does in the same way. 20 For the Father dearly loves the Son and shows Him everything that He Himself is doing; and the Father will show Him greater works than these, so that you will be filled with wonder. (John 5:19-21)***

> ***know a man in Christ who fourteen years ago—whether in the body I do not know, or out of the body I do not know, [only] God***

knows—such a man was caught up to the third heaven. And I know that such a man—whether in the body or out of the body I do not know, [only] God knows— was caught up into]Paradise and heard inexpressible words which man is not permitted to speak [words too sacred to tell]. (2 Corinthians 12:2-4)

The Apostle John Revelation 4:1 –

After this I looked, and behold, a door standing open in heaven! And the first voice which I had heard, like the sound of a [war] trumpet speaking with me, said, "Come up here, and I will show you what must take place after these things."

The voice of our Lord is still beckoning to us even now, "COME UP HERE" come up to a higher level of thinking a Heaven to earth perspective which opens up our spirit man to naturally see this NEW WORLD. This is not a place we go but where we are already seated. It is not a futuristic place it is NOW. This New World is not bound by space and time...but in Christ.

Begin to pray for a stillness inside your inner man that awakens you to seeing and realizing this reality. Eyes to open, eyes to see, eyes to perceive.

Psalms 146:8 says:

> ***The LORD opens the eyes of the blind; The LORD raises up those who are bowed down; The LORD loves the righteous; (BLESSED ARE THE POOR IN SPIRIT FOR THEY WILL SEE GOD)***
>
> ***Then their eyes were opened and they recognized Him; and He vanished from their sight. (Luke 24:31)***

The ability to use all spiritual senses is

imperative for effective prayer

What are the courts of heaven?

- A place to resolve legal issues
- a higher technology released to us as sons to engaged God the righteous judge
- a more effective (quick results) way to pray

The Bible says in Psalm 84:10:

> ***For a day in Your courts is better than a thousand [anywhere else]; ...***

Many of us have been praying about issues for years that have not come to pass because it is not yet its appointed time. However, many have been going around the mountain for years because prayer has been taught as one sided way of communicating. Instead of an interactive higher technology where you come to God the

Father as the righteous judge, Jesus our Big Brother as our Advocate our Lawyer and Our Most Intimate Friend Holy Spirit, who reminds us, leads us, reveals to us legal accusations against us in the Spirit.

We said before, that earth is just a pattern of this world. Jesus said it this way, as it is in heaven so it is on earth. As there are armies in heaven so it is on earth, as there are schools of the Spirit in Heaven in the same way we have schools here on earth. As there are courts here in Heaven to resolve legal issues so there is on earth. I deliberately wrote from Heaven to earth to show us that what we see in the earth gives us clues about what is in Heaven.

The courts of Heaven are a part of this New World. Jesus when He taught His disciples to pray encouraged us to be relentless, persistent in our prayers and never give up. Many, have interpreted that as praying tirelessly rather than praying effectively. That is, allowing the Holy Spirit to reveal what the accusations are against you so that you can repent by the renewing of your mind and becoming one with the mind of Christ. Jesus promised us if we would be persistent we would be avenged quickly.

In Luke 18:1-8:

> ***Now Jesus was telling the disciples a parable to make the point that at all times they ought to pray and not give up and lose heart, saying, "In a certain city there was a judge who did not fear God and had no respect for man. There was a [desperate] widow in that city and she kept coming to him and saying, 'Give me justice and legal protection from my adversary.' For a time, he would not; but later he said to himself, 'Even though I do not fear God nor respect man, yet because this widow continues to bother me, I will give her***

> ***justice and legal protection; otherwise by continually coming she [will be an intolerable annoyance and she] will wear me out.'" Then the Lord said, "Listen to what the unjust judge says! And will not [our just] God defend and avenge His elect [His chosen ones] who cry out to Him day and night? Will He delay [in providing justice] on their behalf? I tell you that He will defend and avenge them quickly. However, when the Son of Man comes, will He find [this kind of persistent] faith on the earth?"***

The parable depicts an unjust judge who neither feared God nor respected man but the bible said that BUT because of the widow's persistence she got her breakthrough. Jesus came and revealed to us that when we pray we are coming before a LOVING FATHER. We say 'Our Father in Heaven' prayer brings us before our Daddy, Abba who instantly brings His Kingdom to earth and meet our needs as we forgive the debts of those whom we think owe us. We see this description in Luke 11:1-4:

> ***"When you pray; say:***
> ***Father, hallowed be Your name.***
> ***Your kingdom come.***
> ***'Give us each day our daily bread***
> ***'And forgive us our sins,***
> ***For we ourselves also forgive everyone who is indebted to us [who has offended or wronged us].***
> ***And lead us not into temptation but rescue us from evil.'"***

So we see here that forgiveness by way of repentance is a key component to our needs being met and the Kingdom coming on earth.

Matthew 5:25 says:

> "***Come to terms quickly [at the earliest opportunity] with your opponent at law while you are with him on the way [to court], so that your opponent does not hand you over to the***

> ***judge, and the judge to the guard, and you are thrown into prison."***

The enemy of our souls is a legalist and so the bible encourages us to settle matters quickly with our adversaries. When we do that Heaven comes to earth as it keeps the heaven open over our lives.

In order for us to settle matters quickly we need to know what is holding back our answered prayers. We see a similar example in Daniel 10 where Daniel's prayer was heard by God the Righteous Judge and yet his words caused a conflict and the answer was held back ark angel Michael came to Daniel's aid and these were his words to him.

> ***"Do not be afraid, "Daniel, for from the first day that you set your heart on understanding this and on humbling yourself before your***

God, your words were heard, and I have come in response to your words. But the prince of the kingdom of Persia was standing in opposition to me for twenty-one days. Then, behold, Michael, one of the chief [of the celestial] princes, came to help me, for I had been left there with the kings of Persia. Now I have come to make you understand what will happen to your people in the latter days, for the vision is in regard to the days yet to come." (Daniel 10:12-14)

WHY HAD NOTHING HAPPENED?

Legal issues...prevent the answers to our prayers.

- WHAT ARE THE LEGALITIES? This could be iniquities from generations before so the need to believe in our entire salvation so that we are not continually being accused of bloodline issues.

- THE COURTS ARE NOT FOR PLEADING AND BEGGING IT IS TO PRESENT YOUR CASE WITH THE DESIRE TO KNOW WHAT THE ACCUSATIONS ARE AND TO REPENT, BY ALIGNING YOUR WILL TO HIS WILL.

The courts are an excellent example of what it looks like when we live from heaven, live from the Heavenly Places, live from this New World every other realm below this realm has to submit to the rule of the highest place, the dwelling place of the Most High God. In the natural world, here on earth, the Supreme Court is the highest court of appeal in the United Kingdom, if this court rules or releases a verdict of not guilty, despite what the Magistrates court says, the Crown court, County court the verdict remains the same. When we are operating from Heaven all verdicts are final it over rules everything on the earth.

PARADIGM SHIFT ACTIVATION

Begin to engage with the courts in heaven by faith.

Here is an example of what the courts look like:-

"I kept looking
Until thrones were set up,
And the Ancient of Days (God) took His seat;
His garment was white as snow
And the hair of His head like pure wool.
His throne was flames of fire;
Its wheels were a burning fire.
"A river of fire was flowing
And coming out from before Him;
A thousand thousands were attending Him,
And ten thousand times ten thousand were standing before Him;
The court was seated,
And the books were opened.

- The NEW WORLD shift requires a heaven to earth perspective
- The use of all your spiritual senses
- A shift from religion to relationship
- Live a life of repentance

By Faith step into the courts of heaven and honor all you see. The Righteous Judge (Father), The Son and The Holy Spirit, angels, seven spirits, the elders. Present your case to your Father the Righteous Judge and ask the Holy Spirit what are the accusations, and call forth the accusers or the negative spirits that need to be called forth to be judged as they are being judged begin to repent as the Holy Spirit reveal to you the accusation. When you spiritually sense you have repented of all accusation ask for a verdict. The verdict is your confession, your declaration, your Word, your weapon against the enemy. Expect change quickly, as promised in Luke 18.

In this New World everything is above and so as we practice to live our lives always from above not below, take all matters to highest place, behind the veil we will begin to see HIS KINGDOM ON EARTH ON A DAILY BASIS.

> ***"For we MUST ALL appear before the judgment seat of Christ that each one may receive what is due him for the things done while in the body, whether good or bad" (2 Corinthians 5:10)***

So why wait until the day of judgment? Why not actively persistently live a lifestyle of repentance through prayer silencing every accusation of the enemy by being blameless in all things and keeping our hearts unveiled.

[redacted]

CHAPTER 5

A NEW WAY OF LIVING

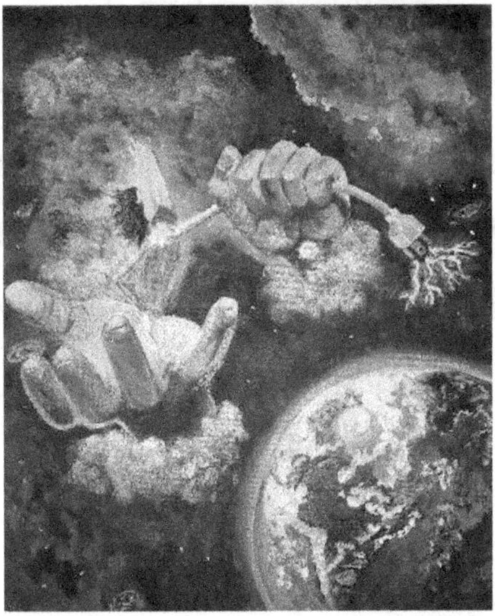

"THE LORD WOULD HAVE YOU KNOW, HIDING OUT IN LODEBAR IS LIVING "BELOW THE BAR". YOU ARE MEANT TO DINE AT THE KING'S TABLE."

~ PAMELA JONES

I grew up in Jamaica, where we are encouraged, beaten, chastised, to be successful as the world deems success. Worldly standards stipulate that success is achieved by our hard work, for many of us by manipulating others, trying to execute our own plans, ambition being the driving force sometimes, even at the cost of others feelings and position. Proverbs 19:21 tells us:

> "***Many plans are in a man's mind, But it is the Lord's purpose for him that will stand (be carried out).***"

This scripture tells me that only the Lord's purpose will prevail so if we are purposing what He has not purposed it will fail. It is not based on our hard work nor how well we schemed but more about being aligned with His will.

As we shift to a new way of living we must

realize that

> ***before He formed us in the womb He knew us (Jeremiah 1:5).***

Ephesians 2:10 says:

> ***For we are his workmanship, created in Christ Jesus for good works, which God prepared beforehand, that we should walk in them.***

This scripture tells us that even what we should be doing while on earth was prepared beforehand and since He knew us while we were unformed then, He would have put in us or befitted us with all we needed to fulfill the good works. We were created '***in Christ Jesus for good works.'*** This tells me these works He created for us to do can only be done in CHRIST JESUS. If we are still in our old man, our flesh, it is impossible to accomplish what He has purposed. To Shift we must first get to a place where we no longer desire our wants, just His.

> ***"But I do not consider my life as something of value or dear to me, so that I may [with joy] finish my course and the ministry which I received from the Lord Jesus, to testify faithfully of the good news of God's [precious, undeserved] grace [which makes us free of the guilt of sin and grants us eternal life]." (Acts 20:24)***

We must expect that as co-heirs to the throne of God we are Highly Favoured and so our Father's Favour propels us according to His original intention for our lives as the Spirit of God orders our steps. Throughout scripture we see that this new way of living is connected with our Rest in Him, Relationship with Him and our Responsibility by choice. We will start with REST.

REST

As believers in Christ we can rest in our immutable God. When your view of God has SHIFTED from worldly point of view to a Heavenly perspective. Rest becomes a natural conduit for living. We rest in the truth that because He is faithful, immutable, unchanging we can REST in who He is in our lives. Throughout the gospels we can note that when people died as we know death, Jesus would say they are asleep. The scriptures say:

> ***"It is vain for you to rise early, to retire late, to eat the bread of anxious labors— FOR HE GIVES [BLESSINGS] TO HIS BELOVED EVEN IN HIS SLEEP. (Psalm 127:2)***

So, we see that what is produced from anxiety and worry is in vain but He gives blessings to HIS BELOVED EVEN IN HIS SLEEP.

It is in our rest; the blessings are released. We see in Genesis 2:21-22:

> ***"So the Lord God caused a DEEP SLEEP to fall upon Adam; and while he slept, He took one of his ribs and closed up the flesh at that place. And the rib which the Lord God had taken from the man He made (fashioned, formed) into a woman, and He brought her and presented her to the man."***

Adam was multiplied as He slept. The Lord used the rib from Adam to fashioned Eve, suggesting that the woman was in Adam and also that God used pre-existing material in Adam to form Eve but while he slept.

Genesis 15: 12-14:

> ***When the sun was setting, a DEEP SLEEP overcame Abram; and a horror (terror, shuddering fear, nightmare) of great***

> ***darkness overcame him. 13 God said to Abram, "Know for sure that your descendants will be strangers [living temporarily] in a land (Egypt) that is not theirs, where they will be enslaved and oppressed for four hundred years***.

Abram too was in a deep sleep when he received the revelation of the enslavement of his descendants. A prophetic utterance that prepared him and would have made known to him in times of hardship that God had not forsaken him. Revelation while you sleep or rest is reiterated in Psalm 46:10, when it says Be still and know.

In Genesis 28: 11:

> ***And he came to a certain place and stayed overnight there because the sun had set. Taking one of the stones of the place, he put it under his head and lay down there [TO***

SLEEP]. He dreamed that there was a ladder (stairway) placed on the earth, and the top of it reached [out of sight] toward heaven; and [he saw] the angels of God ascending and descending on it [going to and from heaven]. And behold, the Lord stood above and around him and said, "I am the Lord, the God of Abraham your [father's] father and the God of Isaac; I will give to you and to your descendants the land [of promise] on which you are lying. Your descendants shall be as [countless as] the dust of the earth, and you shall spread abroad to the west and the east and the north and the south; and all the families (nations) of the earth shall be blessed through you and your] descendants. Behold, I am with you and will keep [careful watch over you and guard] you wherever you may go, and I will bring you back to this [promised] land; for I will not leave you until I have done what I have promised you."

Jacob is well known to pursue what he desired by way of scheming, manipulating, twisting things, striving no matter the negative consequences. Jacob believed the lie that God helps but I have to do it myself. Here we see that in the midst of his REST or sleep was when he received what he had been striving for all his life. He received transformation from within. He received deliverance from a twisted mindset that cost him everything and received an eternal promise of God for his life.

In this place of Rest is where we hear the voice of God clearly. This requires us to follow the right Voice. When we listen to the right VOICE our lives change into the right way of living. Adam and Eve listened to the wrong voice and was evicted from the garden of God. They received a demotion from a heavenly place to an earthly place. Lot listened to the wrong voice through his natural sight and chose to live in

Zoar near Sodom and Gomorrah putting the life of his family in danger. Moses listened to the wrong voice by way of assumption costing him the privilege of entering the promised land. Abraham listened to the wrong voice and had Ishmael instead waiting for the promised son Isaac. Without cultivating a lifestyle of rest; anxiety, fear, worry will drive us to our own destruction as it silences the VOICE of God in us.

Joshua and Caleb in the midst of trepidation and fear chose to remember the Voice of God and held fast to His promises that they are victors, more than conquerors. Jesus listened to the right voice and He experienced victory after victory as He had no personal agenda. His goal was to be a representative of the Father and that He did without any concerns of how He would be perceived by man. His rest within Himself was to PLEASE THE FATHER FIRST

AND FOREMOST AS HIS ONLY DRIVING FORCE. Who are you here to represent? What is driving you? In this place of rest all impure motives ARE silenced. There are two ways of doing things. You can do it naturally or supernaturally. To do it supernaturally, Rest is a key ingredient.

RELATIONSHIP

Unfortunately, we live a world that advocates a microwave mentality. A quick fix, a quickie, a one-night stand, fast food, and advertises this as normal. However, we see throughout scripture that the entire Kingdom of God is forged by ONENESS. This oneness cannot be a reality without relationship. Recently the Lord has been reiterating by experience and by word that there is no MY, ME, MYSELF nor I in ONENESS. ONENESS by definition implies us, we and our; ONENESS is inclusive. I have been convicted by this over and over again, due to natural language we women have adapted to; when we speak of my children, my car, my house forgetting that in any covenant there is no MY. The MY AND I Mentality isolates others from feeling apart and causes division.

Ultimately, what we must see, is that in our UNION with our God commands that the Kingdom is only able to STAND based on the oneness of relationship. In Mark 3:23-26:

> ***"How can Satan drive out Satan? If a kingdom is divided against itself, that kingdom cannot stand. If a house is divided against itself, that house cannot stand. And if Satan opposes himself and is divided, he cannot stand; his end has come."***

We see here first and foremost that our union with God the Father, God the Son, God the Holy Spirit is imperative. Then our union or our relationship with ourselves (spirit, soul and body) is essential so as to prevent operating from a fragmented view of ourselves so we can stand. It is imperative to all our spirit man to be the driving force as we use our soul and body. To merely embrace one segment of ourselves is to divide ourselves.

"WE ARE TO BE ONE AS THEY ARE ONE" (John 17:22).

God by design has empowered us through relationships. Relationship with God Himself and He shows us how to be one with our self and with all the Heavenly help that He has given us. The entire kingdom of God is knitted together by relationships.

Over the years, the Lord has shown me some special relationships within the Kingdom of Heaven that has changed my way of living. Within the seven Spirits of God that are before the throne of God.

> "***Grace and peace to you from him who is, and who was, and who is to come, and from the seven spirit before his throne" (Revelations 1:4)***

> ***From the throne came flashes of lightning, rumblings and peals of thunder. In front of the throne, seven lamps were blazing. These are the seven spirit of God (Revelations 4:5).***

> ***"Then I saw a Lamb, looking as if it had been slain, standing at the center of the throne, encircled by the four living creatures and the elders. The Lamb had seven horns and seven eyes, which are the seven spirits of God sent out into all the earth." (Revelation 5:6)***

We see that these seven spirits are always together which speaks of their interlocking relationship. They are before the throne so they are witnesses of all that happens in the throne room. They greet the churches and they are sent out into the earth. Overtime of seeing how these Spirits work in my life, I have seen that the Spirit of the Fear of the Lord helps us to balance our knowledge (given by the Spirit of knowledge) and understanding (given by the Spirit of Understanding) of God with awe and reverence which ultimately helps us to apply wisdom. Proverbs 1:7 reiterates that:

> "***The fear of the Lord is the beginning of knowledge but fools despise wisdom and instruction.***"

Knowledge without the fear of the Lord only puffs up and causes us to speak folly wisdom of man. You see understanding the relationship between the Spirits helps us in our walk with God.

In my years of being in ministry, miracles

always occur when I partnered with the Spirit of Counsel and the Spirit of Might. That is, I seek out the heart of God through His counsel and apply His counsel, it releases the Spirit of Might to heal, deliver, raise the dead and to release the miraculous. The seven Spirits are sent in the earth to help us as a part of our entourage of Heavenly help but if we cannot honor the relationship they share and apply them appropriately we will be disarmed of authority, power and effectiveness.

Understanding how to relate to angels is also imperative. We notice throughout scripture angels appear and spoke with humans. There was a natural connection. The bible tells us they are ministering spirits, or representatives of God sent by God to minister to us. WOW! A mouthful. When we think of being a representative it suggests you take the place of another. For example, the Apostle Paul writes that we are ambassadors of Christ or representatives of Christ Himself. We see this reinforced in many ways, Jesus said in Matthew 25:35-40:

> ***For I was hungry and you gave me something to eat, I was thirsty and you gave me something to drink, I was a stranger and you invited me in, I needed clothes and you clothed me, I was sick and you looked after me, I was in prison and you came to visit me.' "Then the righteous will answer him, 'Lord, when did we see you hungry and feed you, or thirsty and give you something to drink? When did we see you a stranger and invite you in, or needing clothes and clothe you? When did we see you sick or in prison and go to visit you?'***
>
> ***"The King will reply, 'Truly I tell you, whatever you did for one of the least of these brothers and sisters of mine, you did for me.'***

Jesus demonstrates to us that He sees no difference between us and Himself. When we do for others we are doing for Jesus. He sees us as Himself, representatives of Him. In acts 9: 3-5:

> "***we see another example of Jesus appearing to Saul as he neared Damascus on his journey, suddenly a light from heaven flashed around him. He fell to the ground and heard a voice say to him, "Saul, Saul, why do you persecute me?" "Who are you, Lord?" Saul asked. "I am Jesus, whom you are persecuting," He replied."***

Again, Jesus makes it clear to Saul and to all of us, that what we do to others we are doing to Him be it negative or positive. This reveals how Jesus sees the relationship we have with Him. WE ARE ONE, THERE IS NO I NOR ME. ONE FOR ALL, ALL FOR ONE.

In applying this oneness principle to the angelic as representatives of God sent to us, we must all see that when God speaking through an angel or a man the message is still from God. Therefore, how we relate and perceive the messenger, will determine our ability to receive the message. How are you relating with the angels assigned to you? Let's look at the difference between Mary and Zechariah of how they received the message sent by the same angel.

> ***Then an angel of the Lord appeared to him, standing at the right side of the altar of incense. When Zechariah saw him, he was startled and was gripped with fear. But the angel said to him: "Do not be afraid, Zechariah; your prayer has been heard. Your wife Elizabeth will bear you a son, and you are to call him John. He will be a joy and delight to you, and many will rejoice because of his birth, for he will be great in the sight of***

the Lord. He is never to take wine or other fermented drink, and he will be filled with the Holy Spirit even before he is born. He will bring back many of the people of Israel to the Lord their God. And he will go on before the Lord, in the spirit and power of Elijah, to turn the hearts of the parents to their children and the disobedient to the wisdom of the righteous—to make ready a people prepared for the Lord." Zechariah asked the angel, "How can I be sure of this? I am an old man and my wife is well along in years. The angel said to him, "I am Gabriel. I stand in the presence of God, and I have been sent to speak to you and to tell you this good news. And now you will be silent and not able to speak until the day this happens, because you did not believe my words, which will come true at their appointed time." (Luke 1: 11-20)

Compared to Mary when the angel Gabriel appeared to her.

God sent the angel Gabriel to Nazareth, a town in Galilee, to a virgin pledged to be married to a man named Joseph, a descendant of David. The virgin's name was Mary. The angel went to her and said, "Greetings, you who are highly favored! The Lord is with you."

Mary was greatly troubled at his words and wondered what kind of greeting this might be. But the angel said to her, "Do not be afraid, Mary; you have found favor with God. You will conceive and give birth to a son, and you are to call him Jesus. He will be great and will be called the Son of the Most High. The Lord God will give him the throne of his father David, and he will reign over Jacob's descendants forever; his kingdom will never end."

"How will this be," Mary asked the angel, "since I am a virgin?" The angel answered, "The Holy Spirit will come on you, and the power of the Most High will overshadow you.

> ***So the holy one to be born will be called the Son of God. Even Elizabeth your relative is going to have a child in her old age, and she who was said to be unable to conceive is in her sixth month. For no word from God will ever fail.“ I am the Lord's servant," Mary answered. "May your word to me be fulfilled." Then the angel left her. (Luke 2:27-38)***

Zechariah was afraid when he saw the angel and after much description of his son what he would be named, what he would drink, the purpose of his coming Zechariah still doubted the angel Gabriel.

> "***Zechariah asked the angel, "How can I be sure of this? I am an old man and my wife is well along in years." The angel said to him, "I am Gabriel. I stand in the presence of God, and I have been sent to speak to you and to tell you this good news."***

Zechariah's unbelief caused the angel to mute

him until he would believe.

On the other Hand, when we look at Mary's response. She was humbled by the greeting she received. She certainly did not perceive herself as someone who was Highly favored, and may have not had the revelation that the Lord is with her. The words from the angel Gabriel troubled her scripture says. Again, like Zechariah, Gabriel told her about the Son she would carry from the descendants of Jacob and that He would reign over the throne of David where His Kingdom will never end. Mary's response was how would this be since she was a virgin and the Gabriel built her faith by sharing the testimony of her cousin Elizabeth and Mary shared with the angel how she viewed herself she admitted "I am the servant of the Lord." As she accepted that no word from the Lord will ever fail. She then concluded "May your word to me be fulfilled."

What we see here is that they both had a conversation with an angel and yet Zechariah's questions where fueled by unbelief and a demand for evidence while Mary's attitude was one of a willing servant ready to heed the word of the Lord concerning her. Again I believe the way Mary related to the angel is an example to us of how we too can heed the help that is sent to us from heaven be it an angel, cloud of witness, man in white linen, seven spirits. It is more about understanding that our God always works through relationship and He wants us to treat the words of His representatives just as if He appeared to us. Oneness does not see I and my but us all the time.

Recently in a night vision I received, a friend appeared and gave me two yods (number 10 in Hebrew) and a treasure chest. As I was awakened, I asked the Lord what this meant and His response was from My Heart to your heart. I was flabbergasted because He did not appear but a friend of mine did. Again, she was His messenger and He was reiterating my point that His messenger is a representative of Himself.

PARADIGM SHIFT ACTIVATION

Begin to see yourself always from above and not beneath. When you have God's perspective it quietens all fear, all worry, all doubt because you can see from His eyes and so it releases peace. Cultivate a life of rest and peace.

Cultivate relationship first and foremost with God asking Him questions in humility as He pursues you. Open your mind to the array of ways He can send you help and recognize the oneness He shares with His messengers. Adapt an attitude of a servant, ready to serve, ready to obey.

CHAPTER 6

NEW SOUND

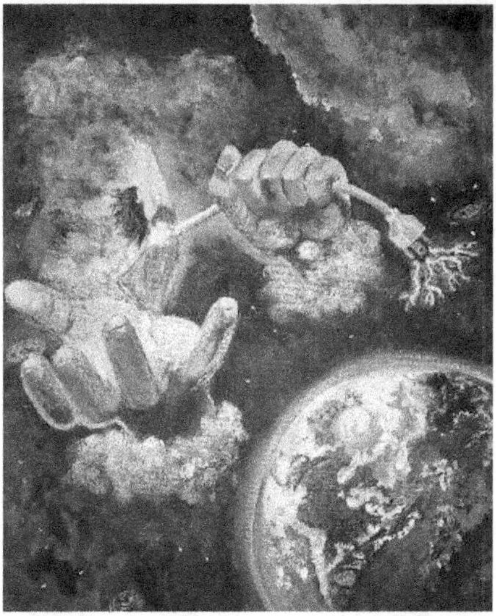

"ALIGNMENT WITH THE SOUND OF HEAVEN CREATES THE SAME VIBRATIONS ON EARTH."

~ CHRISTINE NELSON

We are created to release the sounds of heaven and to be the reflection of His glory. Heaven carries its own frequency, when we come into oneness with its sound the earth reflects the same frequency. His Sound changes our DNA, spiritual environment, as heavens constructs the world, the very atmosphere.

In the realms of the spirit there is no language but a cry a sound. This sound of Heaven prepares our body to shift and change. The whole body and structure are being changed this is called transfiguration. Light and sound comes from the same source; God Himself. When we listen to the heartbeat of the Father, it allows our heart to vibrate simultaneously to His heart. A sound can destroy and a sound can create.

In the beginning, we see that it was a sound

that God used to create the world. Genesis 1: 1-5:

> ***"In the beginning God Elohim created by forming from nothing the heavens and the earth. The earth was formless and void or a waste and emptiness, and darkness was upon the face of the deep primeval ocean that covered the unformed earth. The Spirit of God was moving (hovering, brooding) over the face of the waters. And God said "Let there be light"; and there was light. God saw that the light was good (pleasing, useful) and He affirmed and sustained it; and God separated the light distinguishing it from the darkness. And God called the light day, and the darkness He called night. And there was evening and there was morning, one day."***

We see from this passage that when God is creating something from nothing, as the Holy Spirit broods, the sound of heaven is released and creation happens. The brooding of the Holy

Spirit has a sound and it has a frequency. In fact, EVERYTHING HAS A FREQUENCY. WHEN WE COME INTO ALIGNMENT WITH IT THE FREQUENCY in the wall we can walk through it.

There is another example like this in scripture when Mary was visited by the Angel Gabriel.

> ***"Listen carefully: you will conceive in your womb and give birth to a son, and you shall name Him Jesus. He will be great and eminent and will be called the Son of the Most High; and the Lord God will give Him the throne of His father David; and He will reign over the house of Jacob (Israel) forever, and of His kingdom there shall be no end." Mary said to the angel, "How will this be, since I am a virgin and have no intimacy with any man?" Then the angel replied to her, "THE HOLY SPIRIT WILL COME UPON YOU, AND THE POWER OF THE MOSTHIGH WILL OVERSHADOW YOU [LIKE A CLOUD];***

> ***FOR THAT REASON THE HOLY (PURE, SINLESS) CHILD SHALL BE CALLED THE SON OF GOD. And listen, even your relative Elizabeth has also conceived a son in her old age; and she who was called barren is now in her sixth month. For with God nothing [is or ever] shall be impossible." (Luke 2: 31-37)***

We see that Mary was a virgin and had had no intimate relations. Yet as the Holy Spirit overshadowed her or brood over her with the sound through words released by the angel, our Savior was conceived. God creates something out of nothing by coming into oneness with the frequency or sound that is released by the overshadowing or the brooding of the Holy Spirit. The question is always, what is the Holy Spirit doing and becoming one with that sound. As we become one with sound creation occurs. There is tremendous power in the sounds from heaven and when we come into agreement with the sound of heaven the restoration of all things is here as we vibrate according to the frequencies of His heart. AS HIS HUMAN SHOFARS Aligning with His Sound, breakthrough, restoration, retribution becomes natural.

God's voice is a vibration that holds all things around the world. Hebrews 1:3 –

> ***The Son is the radiance and only expression of the glory of [our awesome] God [reflecting God's Shekinah glory, the Light-being, the brilliant light of the divine], and the exact representation and perfect imprint of His [Father's] essence, and UPHOLDING AND MAINTAINING AND PROPELLING ALL THINGS [THE ENTIRE PHYSICAL AND SPIRITUAL UNIVERSE] BY HIS POWERFUL WORD [CARRYING THE UNIVERSE ALONG TO ITS PREDETERMINED GOAL]. When He [Himself and no other] had [by offering Himself on the cross as a sacrifice for sin] accomplished purification from sins and***

established our freedom from guilt, He sat down [revealing His completed work] at the right hand of the Majesty on high [revealing His Divine authority]

Everything has a vibration and God upholds us by His very Word. GOD IS RELEASING US FROM THE GRAVITATIONAL PULL OF THIS WORLD. This is the Big Shift we speak of. There is great expectation, as all creation is waiting for the sons of God to be unveiled by maturation. In Romans 8:19-25:

For [even the whole] creation [all nature] waits eagerly for the children of God to be revealed. For the creation was subjected to frustration and futility, not willingly [because of some intentional fault on its part], but by the will of Him who subjected it, in hope that the creation itself will also be freed from its bondage to decay [and gain entrance] into the glorious freedom of the children of God. FOR WE KNOW THAT THE WHOLE

> ***CREATION HAS BEEN MOANING TOGETHER AS IN THE PAINS OF CHILDBIRTH UNTIL NOW. AND NOT ONLY THIS, BUT WE TOO, WHO HAVE THE FIRST FRUITS OF THE SPIRIT [A JOYFUL INDICATION OF THE BLESSINGS TO COME], EVEN WE GROAN INWARDLY, AS WE WAIT EAGERLY FOR [THE SIGN OF] OUR ADOPTION AS SONS—THE REDEMPTION AND TRANSFORMATION OF OUR BODY [AT THE RESURRECTION]. FOR IN THIS HOPE WE WERE SAVED [BY FAITH]. But hope [the object of] which is seen is not hope. For who hopes for what he already sees? But if we hope for what we do not see, we wait eagerly for it with patience and composure.***

The creation is waiting for sons of God to arise and mature as they take their rightful place. This is the transformation as we eagerly wait for the sign of our adoption as Sons. You see, from the beginning it was always about a sound through a voice. Throughout scripture we see there are three main levels of voices which even today we can settle for and refrain from attaining.

VOICE OF PLEASURE

This is an instinctual voice, it entices you based on what it looks like and taste like It is all about pleasure. This voice has the ability to drown out even the voice of God. It consumes your mind as it fills you with desire turned to lust and then believing the ultimate lie that you need this pleasure to survive at the expense of your own destruction. This pleasure can be both positive or negative. For example:- Eating a meal for pleasure is fine but no this is not always the case as in the garden of Eden.

This voice of pleasure is the voice that lured Eve in the garden. It was the same voice that spoke through Eve and lured Adam as well. Though they were warned of their impending death if they consumed the fruit from that tree, the Voice of God was silenced as they reasoned away the only Voice that could save them. The voice of pleasure, is full of logical reasons that makes sense to the natural mind. It steals what you once believed in a second. It reminds me of the of the parable of the sower. The seeds that fell on rocky soil.

> "***Other seed fell on rocky ground, where they did not have much soil; and at once they sprang up because they had no depth of soil. But when the sun rose, they were scorched; and because they had no root, they withered away." (Matthew 13:5-6)***

You see, in making the shift one must forsake human reasoning, by being deliberate to meditate on the what God said which creates greater depth of conviction.

This voice reminds me of a poem I wrote many years, as I began to discern between this voice and other voices. The poem is entitled Reasoning.

REASONING

Reasoning is my mind at work trying to explain spiritual things in a physical way.

Reasoning is a peace stealer, Reasoning says what you know to be wrong is right.

Reasoning is a faith stealer. It steals the Word from your hearts and gives the facts.

Reasoning is satan's tool to cause confusion and distraction. Say NO to reasoning and yes to God's Word and obedience peace-faith will keep satan under your feet.

(Written by C Nelson)

EXTERNAL VOICE

The external voice highlights the commands of God, and reinforces right from wrong: it guides us in practical everyday issues – when we practice listening to this voice we attune ourselves to a higher level of vibration (sound) opening us to a higher and a more godly vision. It enables us to see the world through a spiritual reality. The more we obey this voice is the more we are trained in obedience which enables us develop greater depth of character. Romans 5: 3-5 says it this way*:*

> ***And not only this, but [with joy] let us exult in our sufferings and rejoice in our hardships, knowing that hardship (distress, pressure, trouble) produces patient endurance; and endurance, proven character (spiritual maturity); and proven character, hope and confident assurance [of eternal salvation]. Such hope [in God's promises] never disappoints us, because God's love***

has been abundantly poured out within our hearts through the Holy Spirit who was given to us.

The external voice not only reveals the character of God as you obey Him, as it builds His character in you and reveals His depth, even when you don't want to obey.

On the flip side, this voice can sometimes cause us to become robotic. It can cause us to listen to a familiar Spirit of religion that seeks to condemn us rather than to seek out the heart of God looking through His eyes. It was the voice of God that told Hosea to marry a prostitute, It was the voice of God that told Abraham to sacrifice his only Son. This tells us that the external voice though it may not sound like what religion has advocated that God would say, it may be God. God is not operating out of earthly logic and hence the reason why you could miss

His voice or His sound if you are going by the simplicity of right and wrong. I remember in the recent run up to the 2016 US Elections when I heard some of what Donald Trump was saying from the peripheral I began to say negative things against him. In an instant, the Lord silenced me and spoke firmly to me saying 'how dare you speak of Donald Trump without asking Him who is He (God) is planning on using. ' Suffice to say, I learnt then and continue to learn that everything that looks good is not good and equally not everything that looks bad is bad. However, it is imperative to seek out the perspective of the Father. His perspective is always wholesome. It encompasses hindsight, foresight, oversight and insight unlike our human perspective which is limited.

COMPLEX VOICE

This is a more complex voice or a more involved, elaborate, impenetrable voice that is acquired by learning and imbued with humility. This voice is versatile. It knows it can interrupt you whenever, wherever. It is a sound that displaces the darkness when you hear it you know, because it causes your Spirit man to stand at attention. This sound forces us not to judge based on what we hear nor see but to become aware of where we are seated in the Heavenly places and to discern only from a heaven to earth perspective forsaking all other views. This voice or sound knows that our hearts are corrupted and so our God seeks to restore by using light to displace the darkness. Quantum physics is the construction of the sum of all things and this is where we are going. Just like the Spirit of man came out of God and was established in the earth. Let there be light! By Sound, light travels by waves shifting us.

Leaving us without a doubt with NEW REVELATION from the throne of grace.

You see, words, whether spoken or read, brings an image. If I said to you see a van .... you would not see CAR but you would see a van. A Word is frequency. The first frequency God released was "Let there be light." And Boom that frequency caused the creation of all things. He is using that same frequency today, the frequency of light to bring the RESTORATION of all things as the, HOLY SPIRIT BROODS OVER. You see, IN THE REALMS OF THE SPIRIT THERE IS ONLY SOUND. Although, God can only speak to us in a way that we can understand, using words, which is a form of sound. Sound and light move by waves, we travel by electromagnetic waves. We can only see about 3%, and what we see and hear we naturally interpret, according to the paradigms we have been taught, experiences we have had, the wounds we carry and so on. This Shift requires us to apply SOUND ALIGNMENT TO EVERY AREA OF OUR LIVES. IT IS ABOUT FOLLOWING THE SOUND OF GOD, not our own sound, or anyone else's but His sound to us. His Sound carries HIS DNA and as a result reveals His DNA in us. To follow His Sound not only gives us His result but it restores our Light as we are transfigured into His very image as we follow His blueprint to us. To align with God's Sound brings forth God's provision in our lives, establishes God's will on the earth as it helps us overcome delays, roadblocks, lack, and strife in fulfilling God's vision for us. There is a sound coming from heaven. We need to not presume nor assume but rather inquire of Him WHO we align ourselves with and HOW and WHEN so as to fulfill the mission He has given us on earth.

Last year about this time, I was sitting in my

sitting room writing away, when I became aware that the frequency in my living room changed. I looked up and saw a luminous light swiftly moved across the room. I knew it was an angel. I asked 'who are you and why are you here?' I instantly heard Luca. I noticed that the frequency he was releasing was causing my head to ache. The fact that I was in pain made me wonder whether this was from God. You see, I believed the lie that says if it does not look good, feel good and causes pain it is not from God. That's deception. I looked up the meaning of his name and interestingly, his name means luminous. I was floored with awe and wonder. I decided to put all judgments aside and see what unfolded. A few days later, he appeared by my bedside. I asked again why are you here? He told me that he was sent to teach me about frequencies, vibrations and Sound. Well I remember, swallowing in disbelief since I was such a poor science student. I thought he is going to have it hard, because my brain does not even like the word science. Well a year later, to see the growth is awe-inspiring. I am able to sense uncertainty in a voice, even if there is a slightest change in vibration, pick up on atmospheric changes be it a terrorist attack, a riot, peace and so on. I am still learning but that sensitivity that has been revealed in me is amazing and I can't really say what happened than by His grace I remained teachable and humble. I am now so grateful for God sending me this wonderful angel who has partnered with me and ministered to me in this area.

I shared that to say that whatever we partake of determines how our heart works, our kidney works. The sounds we partake of either causes us turmoil or peace. When we partake of anything that does not edify our soul we are choosing to be derailed from hearing the Sound of God. 1 Peter 3:11 says:

> ***"He must turn away from wickedness and do what is right. He must search for peace [with God, with self, with others] and pursue it eagerly [actively—not merely desiring it].***

If we are not operating out of the peace of God we cannot have peace with ourselves nor others.

The enemy of our souls still works through our old man. When we consult the old man, we cannot hear the Sound of God. There are few peace stealers that I would like to I mention: -

- OFFENCE
- ENTITLEMENT

The Pharisee in Luke 18:9-14 thought of himself as someone who was entitled based on his right behavior and he walked in offence towards others who did not. Let's read***...***

"He also told this parable to some people who trusted in themselves and were confident that they were righteous [posing outwardly as upright and in right standing with God], and who viewed others with contempt: "Two men went up into the temple [enclosure] to pray, one a Pharisee and the other a tax collector. The Pharisee stood [ostentatiously] and began praying to himself [in a self-righteous way, saying]: 'God, I thank You that I am not like the rest of men—swindlers, unjust (dishonest), adulterers—or even like this tax collector. I fast twice a week; I pay tithes of all that I get.' But the tax collector, standing at a distance, would not even raise his eyes toward heaven, but was striking his chest [in humility and repentance], saying, 'God, be merciful and gracious to me, the [especially wicked] sinner [that I am]!' I tell you, this man went to his home justified [forgiven of the guilt of sin and placed in right standing with God] rather than the other man; for everyone who exalts

> ***himself will be humbled, but he who humbles himself [forsaking self-righteous pride] will be exalted."***

You can see from this parable that "being offensive" and "being offended" have the same root -- self! I believe, there are two kinds of selfish people those with a self-centered attitude, those that disregard the feelings of others.

Those with a self-problem who also exists with the individual who, though they may seem to be more considerate and unselfish, are still easily offended. Their motives being self-induced that is not led by the Spirit.

WATCH OUT FOR THESE THOUGHTS OR STATEMENTS

- "I didn't get my way..."
- "He was rude to me..."

- "After all I did they didn't even thank me..."
- "I don't get any recognition around here..."
- "He didn't shake my hand..."
- "He took advantage of me..."
- Feeling sorry for yourself
- "Nobody cares about me...I'm not important."

In reality, offenses are "a violation of self-concerns." These mutterings are not the sign of someone who is dead - a dead man cannot be offended. Offense is a sign that you are seeking out the wrong sound; the sound of the dead. Why? Because...

> ***"I have been crucified with Christ; it is no longer I who live, but Christ lives in me..." (Gal. 2:20).***

When we read this scripture it is clear that this life in Christ we are called to IS NOT A WALKING SIDE BY SIDE WITH CHRIST; THIS IS LIVING THE LIFE OF CHRIST HIMSELF. THE ENEMY CAN ONLY WORK THROUGH THE DEAD; THE OLD MAN.

> ***And you [He made alive when you] were [spiritually] dead and separated from Him because of your transgressions and sins, in which you once walked. You were following the ways of this world [influenced by this present age], in accordance with the prince of the power of the air (Satan), the spirit who is now at work in the disobedient [the unbelieving, who fight against the purposes of God]. Among these [unbelievers] we all once lived in the passions of our flesh [our behavior governed by the sinful self], indulging the desires of human nature [without the Holy Spirit] and [the impulses] of the [sinful] mind. We were, by nature, children [under the sentence] of [God's]***

> ***wrath, just like the rest [of mankind].*** Ephesians 2:2-3

When we are unplugged from the world's view we cut off these passions once and for all.

Where the spirit of entitlement is INGRATITUDE IS PRESENT. GRATITUTDE rooted in humility IS ONE OF THE TOOLS OUR FATHER USES FOR PROMOTION AND EXPANSION. James says:

> ***therefore humble yourselves under the mighty hand of God [set aside self-righteous pride], so that He may exalt you [to a place of honor in His service] at the appropriate time, (1 Peter 5:6)***

WE CAN HAVE AN ENTITLEMENT MENTALITY OR A SERVANTS HEART BUT NOT BOTH.

PARADIGM SHIFT ACTIVATION

To follow the sounds of Heaven we need to:

- Be attuned to GOD's VOICE – by His training.
- Stay in a place of humility before God.
- Consult only God forsake the old you.
- Refuse to make assumptions and presumptions by going by what you see or hear - instead seek out the perspective of God always and align with it.
- In all you do stay in relationship seeking Him with all your heart.
- Ask the Lord if He would assign you an angel to help you to discern His sound in all things.

CHAPTER 7

NEW POSITION AND POSSESSION

"ONE CAN NOT LOSE WHAT HE DOES NOT HOLD ONTO."

~ SILAS VALENTINE

The question is what or who are you tethered to? When you are seated in heavenly places you have all you need. By your position all your needs are met. This mindset shifts from the need to hold on to anyone, or anything as an alternate source but to look to the only true SOURCE!

Christ is your Source, your Salvation, your REAL LIFE, your HOLINESS, your Righteousness, your DNA. Through all your good choices you cannot achieve any of these qualities. You have been given a entirely NEW STATE OF BEING. A tree cannot achieve tree status it was created that way. When you believe that what Jesus has done on the cross is enough, then you know your good behavior cannot make you any more blessed than you are. YOU ARE ONE IN CHRIST You are sitting on the throne of God with Him because you are in Him.

The Tree of good and evil tells us that if you do something wrong, do not expect the blessings of God. When Adam and Eve ate from the fruit from the tree of good and evil, the works of flesh tells us that our good behavior stirs up death, frustration or religious pride. If I have fasted and it works, I go into pride if I fast and nothing happens I fall into condemnation. This system of good and evil is always trying to behave to move the Hand of God while when you do bad you get bad. Jesus came and died so that we did not have to be on this endless roller coaster. Adam and Eve got kicked out of the garden because they used this method to gain possession. They tree of good and evil is the tree that got Adam and Eve evicted from the Heavenly garden. To shift to our God's original intention for our lives, partaking of this tree of good and evil cannot bring us into the reality of the intimacy with God, walking in perfect union. In fact, the tree of good and evil caused spiritual death to both Adam and Eve. For us to regain our state of being the LIGHT we need to unplug from every ulterior source that is masquerading as the tree of good and evil and partake of the only Divine Source, God Himself.

You are either in heaven where you have everything or you are on earth trying to get the blessings from heaven. When you believe this truth that you lack no good thing, striving ceases to be your portion. Religion says you have to work your way up. Christ says I save you so you are already as high as you can be. Where we appeal to determines if we are above or below. The Highest realm is the determining factor of our position as well as what you and I can possess.

Our God loves to work in threes. Throughout scripture we see a consistency in the use of the number three.

- In time there is – *Yesterday, Today, and Tomorrow*
- Our realm of existence is - *Sun, Moon, and Earth*
- God's people are – *Called, Chosen, and Elected*
- History is – *Past, Present, and Future.*
- Our service to God is – *Thought, Word, and Deed.*
- Man is made up of - *Body, Soul, and Spirit.*
- The Godhead is – *Father, Son, and Holy Ghost.*
- Our King's title is –*Lord, Jesus, Christ.*
- There were three areas of worship in the Tabernacle - *The Outer Court, The Holy Place, and the Holy of Holies.*
- Ancient Israel was to appear before God three times each year - *The Feast of*

> *Passover, The Feast of Weeks (Pentecost), and the Feast of Tabernacles.*

The third day is the most mentioned day in the Scriptures. The profound use of the number three reveals God bringing His creation, man, into divine perfection. Examples of these hidden mysteries of God, hidden in the number three can be found in His Word. In his letter to the Hebrews, Paul reveals how Moses was to construct the tabernacle in the wilderness:

> ***"Who serve unto the example and shadow of heavenly things, as Moses was admonished of God when he was about to make the tabernacle: for, they serve as a pattern and foreshadowing of [what has its true existence and reality in] the heavenly things (sanctuary). For when Moses was about to erect the tabernacle, he was warned by God, saying, "See that you make it all [exactly]***

according to the pattern which was shown to you on the mountain. " (Hebrews 8:5)

The heavenly things are the Spiritual Things God revealed to Moses when He gave him the pattern of the Tabernacle in the Wilderness.

What is clear, based on the pattern of tabernacles there are three levels of positioning but only one level that encompasses the abundant life Jesus spoke of. We can work our way up from the outer court to the Holy place and then to the Holy of Holies. However, true Christianity is where the veil is torn and Yahweh comes and lives in our spirit man and the Christ in us flows from our spirit man affecting our soul and then our body. However, religion encourages us to live our lives from the outside in. That is, body, soul and then spirit rather than from our spirit, soul and then our body. THIS BIG SHIFT COMPELS US TO BELIEVE GOD

ONCE AND FOR ALL TO ONLY LIVE FROM OUR SPIRIT MAN, THE HOLY OF HOLIES THE HEAVENLY PLACE. The soul and body only partakes of the Tree of good and evil fruit. THE SPIRIT MAN PARTAKES ONLY OF THE TREE OF LIFE (CHRIST HIMSELF) AND IT RELEASES TO THE SOUL TO THE BODY AND THEN TO THE WORLD.

Below is a table that outlines the different realms. You are born of God. Everything you are told you will have when you die you already have it when Jesus died and you accepted Him you gained access to all He has. THE INVISIBLE REALM is the SUPERIOR REALM. In this invisible realm is the Highest Court, it over rules the inner court and the outer court. **Whatever court you appeal to rules over you.** For example: - If I appeal to the supernatural realm or the inner court and a demon appears to me, I will freak out. However, if you are operating from the invisible realm and a demon begins to speak, you can stay in your place of rest and the demon bows to the higher court. This awesome realm when it is in leading position Heaven comes to Earth and we begin to live as Sons not children under tutors and governors.

Our health for instance, in the physical realm, when sickness knocks at the door, we instantly run to doctors and we take the medicines prescribed to feel better or any alternate medicine. In the supernatural realm you fast and pray and the person is healed. In the Invisible or Heavenly realm, you know there is no sickness in Heaven and so you come into agreement with that truth in spirit, soul and body. By doing so sickness has to leave. This is one area I have struggled with because I have read many health books and have eaten well all my life so the the tree of knowledge good and evil always wants to dictate. However, I have been healed from torn muscles, debilitating chest pains by aligning accordingly.

INVISIBLE REALM	**SUPERNATURAL REALM**	**PHYSICAL REALM**
LOVE is the fuel that sustains or the most excellent way.	Gifts are the fuel that sustains	Gifts, talents, titles education
UNION or ONENESS is the enabling force there is no ME nor I. Relationship	SEPARATION-competitiveness, comparison, they, them, you.	SEPARATION: competitiveness , comparison, they, them, you
In this realm 100-fold increase	60-fold blessing	30-fold blessing
Ecclesia church	Grace church	Traditional church
Governed by INTIMACY/Relationship-Rest e.g.. I only do what I see my Father do.	Governed by achievement, works, titles, e.g.. Apostle, Prophet, teacher, pastor.	Governed by achievement, works,
HOLY OF HOLIES Holy of Holies, Dwelling place of God, Eden, Mercy	Holy Place: Soul of man, Mind, will, emotions, 5 senses, sensual, need the anointing	Outer Court Human being, Body Carnal person

Seat, Spirit of man, SENSITIVE to Anointed One	to operate	
PERFECTION-SON OF GOD finished work. You have all you need. No lack. E.g. Isaac, the fulfillment of the promises of God.	Child under tutors and governors. Striving towards perfection. You are in constant lack and need to meet need. E.g. Ishmael	Attaining perfection, striving. You are in constant lack and need to meet need. E.g. Ishmael
Incorruptible seed, Everything Jesus is, Co-heirs of Christ, DNA of God, MIND OF CHRIST, Substance given freely, immortal	Corruptible seed, generational curses, bloodline cleansing, spiritual mapping (knowing the spiritual history of a region so as to cleanse it), mortal.	Corruptible seed, we live and we die

In the invisible realm, we are a priest and king unto our God. We are sons of God ruling and reigning not a child always beseeching, pleading for help. When you know that your in union or oneness with our Lord and Savior it means all Jesus has you have too, bringing

Heaven to earth becomes a natural lifestyle. As we abandon ourselves to retrain our minds to be a King and Priest unto our God we learn to reign with Him from above.

A King is autonomous; he/she is always above not beneath. He/she takes responsibility for the region, nation, country, city town given and watches over it to ensure it is looks like heaven. If it doesn't, you spontaneously rule and reign as it is in Heaven as you see the Father do. A priest is someone who STANDS in the gap for someone cannot do that for themselves. Someone who intercedes for someone dealing with root issues that are operating as they are lead by the Spirit of God. Operating in our position as King and Priest is natural when we know we are a son of God given the responsibility to be a co-heir with Christ. Our God wants us to be like Him that is why He gave us His DNA. We are perfectly and wonderfully made the same incorruptible seed as Yeshua we are twins with Yeshua. We have the same potential growing into maturity and BE LIKE GOD. Everything you need to be like God He has given it to you and He wants you to do even greater than He did.

Many who are in the supernatural realm are convinced they are in the Holy of Holies. Yet, in this realm you are still partaking of the tree of good and evil. In this realm, you are told you have to behave a certain way, whether through confession, fasting, tithing, this requires a strong headed, striving, self-sufficient perspective. Is this the gospel? Believing and confessing may work but it cannot be replicated. However, when we are in Christ, whatever Christ is, you are. Christ is not sick, nor poor, nor weak so neither are you. The Galatian Christians were rebuked by Paul for going back to the law and works rather than resting in Christ.

> ***"O you foolish and thoughtless and superficial Galatians, who has bewitched you [that you would act like this], to whom—right before your very eyes—Jesus Christ was publicly portrayed as crucified [in the gospel message]? This is all I want to ask of you: did you receive the [Holy] Spirit as the result of obeying [the requirements of] the Law, or was it the result of hearing [the message of salvation and] with faith [believing it]? Are you so foolish and senseless? Having begun [your new life by faith] with the Spirit, are you now being perfected and reaching spiritual maturity by the flesh [that is, by your own works and efforts to keep the Law]?" (Galatians 3:1-3)***

PARADIGM SHIFT ACTIVATION

Refrain from living from earth to heaven but from heaven to earth, no longer outside in but inside out by no longer striving for what is already ours but by REST in the very person, nature of God and belief in His WORD.

MEDITATE ON THESE SCRIPTURES UNTIL THEY BECOME REAL TO YOU, APPLYING THEM, CAUSING THE WORD TO BECOME FLESH AND THE BIG SHIFT BECOMES A NATURAL PARADIGM TO EMBRACE.

Every Spiritual Blessing is in the Heavenly realms in Christ. Ephesians 1:3-6:

> ***Blessed and worthy of praise be the God and Father of our Lord Jesus Christ, who has blessed us with EVERY SPIRITUAL***

BLESSING IN THE HEAVENLY REALMS IN CHRIST, just as [in His love] He chose us in Christ [actually selected us for Himself as His own] before the foundation of the world, so that we would be holy [that is, consecrated, set apart for Him, purpose-driven] and blameless in His sight. In love He predestined and lovingly planned for us to be adopted to Himself as [His own] children through Jesus Christ, in accordance with the kind intention and good pleasure of His will— to the praise of His glorious grace and favor, which He so freely bestowed on us in the Beloved [His Son, Jesus Christ].

Ephesians 1:18-23:

And [I pray] that the eyes of your heart [the very center and core of your being] may be enlightened [flooded with light by the Holy Spirit], so that you will know and cherish the hope [the divine guarantee, the confident expectation] to which He has called you, the riches of His glorious inheritance in the

saints (God's people), and [so that you will begin to know] what the immeasurable and unlimited and surpassing greatness of His [active, spiritual] power is in us who believe. These are in accordance with the working of His mighty strength which He produced in Christ when He raised Him from the dead and seated Him at His own right hand in the heavenly places, far above all rule and authority and power and dominion [whether angelic or human], and [far above] every name that is named [above every title that can be conferred], not only in this age and world but also in the one to come. And He [i]put all things [in every realm] in subjection under Christ's feet, and [j]appointed Him as [supreme and authoritative] head over all things in the church, which is His body, the fullness of Him who fills and completes all things in all [believers]

remember that at that time you were separated from Christ [excluded from any relationship with Him], alienated from the

commonwealth of Israel, and strangers to the covenants of promise [with no share in the sacred Messianic promise and without knowledge of God's agreements], having no hope [in His promise] and [living] in the world without God. But now [at this very moment] in Christ Jesus you who once were [so very] far away [from God] have been brought near by the blood of Christ. FOR HE HIMSELF IS OUR PEACE AND OUR BOND OF UNITY. (Ephesians 2:12-14)

Our Access

For it is through Him that we both have a [direct] way of approach in one Spirit to the Father. So then you are no longer strangers and aliens [outsiders without rights of citizenship], but you are fellow citizens with the saints (God's people), and are [members] of God's household (Ephesians 2:18-19)

True Fellowship with one another is in Him

In Him [and in fellowship with one another] you also are being built together into a dwelling place of God in the Spirit. (Ephesians 2:22)

Son of God our twin…

As He is so are we (1 John 4:17b)

has in these last days spoken [with finality] to us in [the person of One who is by His character and nature] His Son [namely Jesus], whom He appointed heir and lawful owner of all things, through whom also He created the universe [that is, the universe as a space-time-matter continuum]. 3 The Son is the radiance and only expression of the glory of [our awesome] God [reflecting God's Shekinah glory, the Light-being, the brilliant light of the divine], and the exact representation and perfect imprint of His

> ***[Father's] essence, and upholding and maintaining and propelling all things [the entire physical and spiritual universe] by His powerful word [carrying the universe along to its predetermined goal]. When He [Himself and no other] had [by offering Himself on the cross as a sacrifice for sin] accomplished purification from sins and established our freedom from guilt, He sat down [revealing His completed work] at the right hand of the Majesty on high [revealing His Divine authority], (Hebrews 1:2-3)***

Inheriting the promise

> ***For when God made the promise to Abraham, He swore [an oath] by Himself, since He had no one greater by whom to swear, saying, "I will surely bless you and I will surely multiply you." And so, having patiently waited, he realized the promise [in the miraculous birth of Isaac, as a pledge of what was to come from God]. (Hebrews 6:13-15)***

Melchizedek made like the Son of God

For this Melchizedek, king of Salem, priest of the Most High God, met Abraham as he returned from the slaughter of the kings and blessed him, and Abraham gave him a tenth of all [the spoil]. He is, first of all, by the translation of his name, king of righteousness, and then he is also king of Salem, which means king of peace. Without [any record of] father or mother, nor ancestral line, without [any record of] beginning of days (birth) nor ending of life (death), but having been made like the Son of God, he remains a priest without interruption and without successor. (Hebrews 7:1-3)

Better Covenant

who has become a priest, not on the basis of a physical and legal requirement in the Law [concerning his ancestry as a descendant of Levi], but on the basis of the power of an

indestructible and endless life. (Hebrews 7:16)

High Priest able to save completely

The [former successive line of] priests, on the one hand, existed in greater numbers because they were each prevented by death from continuing [perpetually in office]; but, on the other hand, Jesus holds His priesthood permanently and without change, because He lives on forever. THEREFORE HE IS ABLE ALSO TO SAVE FOREVER (COMPLETELY, PERFECTLY, FOR ETERNITY) THOSE WHO COME TO GOD THROUGH HIM, SINCE HE ALWAYS LIVES TO INTERCEDE AND INTERVENE ON THEIR BEHALF [WITH GOD]. (Hebrews 7:23-25)

Sacrifices of the law cannot make perfect

For since the Law has only a shadow [just a pale representation] of the good things to

come—not the very image of those things—it can never, by offering the same sacrifices continually year after year, make [a]perfect those who approach [its altars]. For if it were otherwise, would not these sacrifices have stopped being offered? For the worshipers, having once [for all time] been cleansed, would no longer have a consciousness of sin. But [as it is] these [continual] sacrifices bring a fresh reminder of sins [to be atoned for] year after year, for it is impossible for the blood of bulls and goats to take away sins. (Hebrews 10:1-4)

Sanctified and perfected forever

For by the one offering He has perfected forever and completely cleansed those who are being sanctified [bringing each believer to spiritual completion and maturity]. (Hebrews 10:14)

Access to the Holy of Holies

> ***Therefore, believers, since we have confidence and full freedom to enter the Holy Place [the place where God dwells] by [means of] the blood of Jesus, by this new and living way which He initiated and opened for us through the veil [as in the Holy of Holies], that is, through His flesh, and since we have a great and wonderful Priest [Who rules] over the house of God, let us approach [God] with a true and sincere heart in unqualified assurance of faith, having had our hearts sprinkled clean from an evil conscience and our bodies washed with pure water. (Hebrews 10:19, 22)***

BY OUR OWN CONFESSIONS AND BELIEFS, WE HAVE SHUT THE HEAVENS OR OPEN THE HEAVENS. IT IS TIME TO BELIEVE THE TRUE GOSPEL. JESUS CAME TO REVEAL HIMSELF AS OUR DIVINE PATTERN. HE SHOWED US HOW TO LIVE OUT HIS LIFE

THROUGH ONENESS. AS WE EMBRACE HIS LIFE WE MANIFEST OUR NEW MAN WHICH REVEALS TO US A NEW WORLD, NEW WAY OF THINKING, NEW LEVELS OF AUTHORITY, NEW WAY OF LIVING, A NEW SOUND AND A NEW POSITION THAT ULTIMATELY BRINGS NEW POSSESSION. THE BIG SHIFT IS NO LONGER AN OPTION BUT A NECESSITY. UNPLUGGING FROM THIS EARTH IS CRUCIAL, AS WE LOOK ONLY TO THE TRUE SOURCE, BREAKING FREE FROM ALL ALTERNATE SOURCES ONCE AND FOR ALL.

AUTHOR'S BIOGRAPHY

Christine Nelson is an ordained apostle, prophetic messenger, a sought-after teacher, an international speaker, song writer, mentor, entrepreneur, overseer of CN MINISTRIES. DIRECTOR OF (CNMAEI) CNM Apostolic Equipping Institute where the sons of God are matured, Director of CN Publishers and the author of the Walking in Oneness series.

She is passionate about equipping believers to hear, know, and follow God on a moment by moment experience. She teaches the foundational truth of the Word with simplicity, while revealing deep things of the spirit in practical ways. She has the unique ability to demystify the supernatural side of a real relationship with a living God and make it an accessible reality for all believers. She awakens the desire for believers to embrace their true identity as sons, their divine purpose by engaging the reality of a supernatural God as we become aware of the embodiment of His image in us.

Christine has been married to her best friend, Omowale Nelson, for twenty years, and is the proud mother of their two boys Kobi and Kristian.

OTHER BOOKS BY CHRISTINE NELSON

Taking the Father by the Hand –
Walking in Oneness

Step up and Step in – Oneness Transforms

Seeing yourself through the eyes of Jesus –
Oneness Personifies

Knowing Him in His Glory –
Oneness Reveals His Person

Contend for your Faith –
Oneness Discerns Truth

Reawakening in Him –
Oneness Embodies Christ

Father I never knew- Oneness reveals sons

CHECK OUT OUR ONLINE INSTITUTE

www.cnmaei.com

This institute is unique in many ways. You have full access to it by any device, be it a smart phone, iPad, laptop or a computer with internet access from anywhere in the world.

We do an array of series which come pact with ground breaking teaching, notes, life changing activations, homework and discussions.

Walking in Oneness webinar series

Epic Supernatural Webinar Series - reclaiming the supernatural being you are

Contend for your faith - 7 weeks of taking back what is yours

Champions Arise - Cultivating a heavenly mindset

Biblical Hebrew - Engaging His Words

****

<u>COMING SOON!!!</u>

- The Father I never knew- Being Fathered by the Father
- Understanding the parables from a Hebrew perspective
- Prophetic Course- Raising up throne room prophets
- Every six weeks a one day intensive or online conference

www.ingramcontent.com/pod-product-compliance
Lightning Source LLC
Chambersburg PA
CBHW060835110426
R18122100001BA/R181221PG42736CBX00037BA/47